Weather Tales

Teacher's Guide

Read Well 1 • Unit 36

Critical Foundations in Primary Reading

Marilyn Sprick, Lisa Howard, Ann Fidanque, Shelley V. Jones

ISBN 13-digit: 978-1-59318-459-9 ISBN 10-digit: 1-59318-459-X 132089/2-12

10 11 12 13 RRDHRBVA 15 14 13 12

SOPRIS WEST EDUCATIONAL SERVICES
A CAMBIUM LEARNING COMPANY

BOSTON, MA • LONGMONT, CO

Table of Contents

Unit 36

Weather Tales

Important Tips

How to Teach the Lessons

How to Teach the Lessons (*continued*)

End of the Unit

READ WELL I SEQUENCE AND SOUND PRONUNCIATION GUIDE

I **I** Voiced (Word) **Unit A**	Mm /mmm/ **Monkey** Continuous Voiced **Unit B**	Ss /sss/ **Snake** Continuous Unvoiced **Unit 1**	Ee /eee/ **Emu** Continuous Voiced (Long) **Unit 2**	ee /eeee/ **Bee** Continuous Voiced (Long) **Unit 2**	Mm /mmm/ **Monkey** Continuous Voiced **Unit 3**
Aa /aaa/ **Ant** Continuous Voiced (Short) **Unit 4**	Dd /d/ **Dinosaur** Quick Voiced (not duh) **Unit 5**	th /ththth/ **the** Continuous Voiced **Unit 6**	Nn /nnn/ **Nest** Continuous Voiced **Unit 7**	Tt /t/ **Turkey** Quick Unvoiced (not tuh) **Unit 8**	Ww /www/ **Wind** Continuous Voiced (woo) **Unit 9**
Ii /iii/ **Insects** Continuous Voiced (Short) **Unit 10**	Th /Ththth/ **The** Continuous Voiced **Unit 10**	Hh /h/ **Hippo** Quick Unvoiced (not huh) **Unit 11**	Cc /c/ **Cat** Quick Unvoiced (not cuh) **Unit 12**	Rr /rrr/ **Rabbit** Continuous Voiced **Unit 13**	ea /eaeaea/ **Eagle** Continuous Voiced (Long) **Unit 13**
Sh/sh /shshsh/ **Sheep** Continuous Unvoiced **Unit 14**	Kk, -ck /k/ **Kangaroo** Quick Unvoiced (not kuh) **Unit 15**	oo /oooo/ **Moon** Continuous Voiced (Long) **Unit 16**	ar /ar/ **Shark** Voiced (R-Controlled) **Unit 17**	Wh/wh /wh/ **Whale** Quick Voiced **Unit 18**	Ee /ĕĕĕ/ **Engine or Ed** Continuous Voiced (Short) **Unit 19**
-y /-yyy/ **Fly** Continuous Voiced (Long) **Unit 20**	Ll /lll/ **Letter** Continuous Voiced **Unit 21**	Oo /ooo/ **Otter** Continuous Voiced (Short) **Unit 22**	Bb /b/ **Bat** Quick Voiced (not buh) **Unit 23**	all /all/ **Ball** Voiced **Unit 23**	Gg /g/ **Gorilla** Quick Voiced (not guh) **Unit 24**
Ff /fff/ **Frog** Continuous Unvoiced **Unit 25**	Uu /uuu/ **Umbrella** Continuous Voiced (Short) **Unit 26**	er /er/ **Sister** Voiced (R-Controlled) **Unit 27**	oo /oo/ **Book** Voiced (Short) **Unit 27**	Yy /y-/ **Yarn** Quick Voiced **Unit 28**	Aa /a/ **Ago** Voiced (Schwa) **Unit 28**
Pp /p/ **Pig** Quick Unvoiced (not puh) **Unit 29**	ay /ay/ **Hay** Voiced **Unit 29**	Vv /vvv/ **Volcano** Continuous Voiced **Unit 30**	Qu/qu /qu/ **Quake** Quick Unvoiced **Unit 31**	Jj /j/ **Jaguar** Quick Voiced (not juh) **Unit 32**	Xx /ksss/ **Fox** Continuous Unvoiced **Unit 33**
or /or/ **Horn** Voiced (R-Controlled) **Unit 33**	Zz /zzz/ **Zebra** Continuous Voiced **Unit 34**	a_e /a_e/ **Cake** Bossy E Voiced (Long) **Unit 34**	-y /-y/ **Baby** Voiced **Unit 35**	i_e /i_e/ **Kite** Bossy E Voiced (Long) **Unit 35**	ou /ou/ **Cloud** Voiced **Unit 36**
ow /ow/ **Cow** Voiced **Unit 36**	Ch/ch /ch/ **Chicken** Quick Unvoiced **Unit 37**	ai /ai/ **Rain** Voiced (Long) **Unit 37**	igh /igh/ **Flight** Voiced (Long) **Unit 38**	o_e /o_e/ **Bone** Bossy E Voiced (Long) **Unit 38**	ir /ir/ **Bird** Voiced (R-Controlled) **Unit 38**

Introduction

Weather Tales

Story Notes

Is it fact or fiction? In Unit 35, children learned when someone makes up a story, the story is called fiction. Since zebras don't wear clothes, talk, and have jobs as detectives, "The Case of the Missing Ring" was clearly fiction. In this unit, your students will enjoy trying to determine whether strange stories about frog and fish rain are fact or fiction. What do you think?

Recommended Read Aloud

For reading outside of small group instruction

Cloudy With a Chance of Meatballs by Judi Barrett

Narrative • Problem Solution

The weather in Chewandswallow has always been a bit unpredictable—wind that blows in drifts of cream cheese and jelly sandwiches and tomato tornados. But a storm of pancakes and syrup finally becomes too much for the town. Children love this delicious book with its fun text and hilarious illustrations.

Read Well Connection

Both the *Read Well* stories and *Cloudy With a Chance of Meatballs* are full of delightfully absurd weather images. Since frog and fish rain are factual weather events, perhaps it could rain meatballs!

NOTE FROM THE AUTHORS

As children near the end of the program, take a moment to reflect on all that they have learned in a few short months. Congratulate yourself—and them—on a job well done. Learning to read is not as natural as learning to talk. Helping young children master the reading process requires the support, guidance, and inspiration of caring teachers who recognize that learning to read well is a life-changing experience.

New and Important Objectives

A Research-Based Reading Program

Just Right for Young Children

Oral Language
Phonemic Awareness
Phonics
Fluency
Vocabulary
Comprehension

◆◆ Oral Language

In Units 21–38, language patterns are provided for high-frequency words and for some of the low-frequency words that are likely to require clarification. For English Language Learners and children with language delays, see page 10 for a list of the new high-frequency patterns.

Phonemic Awareness

Isolating Beginning, Middle, Ending Sounds, Segmenting, Blending, Rhyming, Onset and Rime

Phonics

Letter Sounds and Combinations

★*ou*, ★*ow*

★*-ly*

Review • *Ss, Ee, ee, Mm, Aa, Dd, th, Nn, Tt, Ww, Ii, Th, Hh, Cc, Rr, ea, sh, Sh, Kk, -ck, oo, ar, wh, Wh,* e (short), *-y* (as in "fly"), *Ll, Oo, Bb, all, Gg, Ff, Uu, er, oo* (as in "book"), *Yy, a* (schwa), *Pp, ay, Vv, Qq, Jj, Xx, or, Zz, a_e, -y* (as in "baby"), *i_e*

Pattern Words

★*around,* ★*base,* ★*brown,* ★*cars,* ★*clocks,* ★*cloud,* ★*clouds,* ★*cloudy,* ★*clown,* ★*coot,* ★*cow,* ★*dame,* ★*dig,* ★*dogs,* ★*down,* ★*easy,* ★*expected,* ★*fallen,* ★*Falls,* ★*fifty,* ★*flip,* ★*Flip,* ★*flop,* ★*Flop,* ★*flower,* ★*foolishly,* ★*found,* ★*froggy,* ★*frown,* ★*glasses,* ★*grabbed,* ★*Greg,* ★*Greg's,* ★*ground,* ★*groundhog,* ★*groundhogs,* ★*hands,* ★*happened,* ★*happening,* ★*happily,* ★*houses,* ★*how,* ★*How,* ★*However,* *★*indoor,* ★*jitterbugged,* ★*kerplop,* ★*Kerplop,* ★*loud,* ★*lumps,* ★*mound,* ★*mountain,* ★*now,* ★*Now,* ★*oddest,* ★*out,* *★*outdoors,* ★*outfit,* ★*outstanding,* ★*planet,* ★*plenty,* ★*plop,* ★*Plop,* ★*popped,* ★*pound,* ★*power,* ★*quickly,* ★*rabbit's,* ★*really,* ★*round,* ★*safety,* ★*seventy,* ★*shelter,* ★*shout,* ★*shouted,* ★*shower,* ★*Shower,* ★*silly,* ★*sixty,* ★*slip,* ★*slipped,* ★*sound,* ★*sounds,* ★*streets,* ★*strike,* ★*strikes,* ★*struck,* ★*sucked,* ★*summer,* ★*take,* ★*tenderly,* ★*thousands,* ★*torn,* ★*town,* ★*twenty,*

* *Note:* As a pattern is established, a Tricky Word (e.g., "about") will be moved from the Tricky Word category to the Pattern Word category.

◆◆ = Oral language patterns ★ = New in this unit Underline = New words introduced in context

Pattern Words *(continued)*

★*underground,* ★*upon,* ★*wiggle,* ★*winds,* ★*winter,* ★*wow,* ★*Wow*

Review • **about, *About, afternoon, Afternoon, ago, all, along, also, always, am, an, An, and, And, asked, asleep, at, Away, back, backyard, Bats, be, began, block, but, But, called, came, can, Can, can't, cape, cats, clapped, clean, darken, day, Day, detectives, did, dreams, drop, dry, ever, every, fact, Fact, fall, falling, far, fell, fish, Fish, fly, Fly, for, frog, Frog, frogs, Frogs, funny, Go, going, Going, Good, green, Green, gust, had, hard, hats, He, hear, Hear, her, hop, Hop, hopping, hundred, Hundreds, if, If, in, In, it, It, It's, just, Just, lake, landed, leak, lick, like, look, Look, looked, lots, luck, made, make, man, may, Maybe, mud, my, My, never, next, Next, No, not, Not, odd, old, on, or, picked, pig, pigs, Pigs, play, problem, Raccoons, ran, rat, read, real, rings, river, see, See, seem, seen, she, sky, small, smell, so, soon, started, stop, story, Story, Strong, sunny, swish, tell, ten, than, thank, that, That, them, then, Then, thing, things, think, this, too, trees, up, we, wedding, well, Well, whack, Whack, when, When, whether, Why, will, wind, wings, with, years, Yes*

Tricky Words

★*Again,* ★*don't,* ★*English,* ★*everywhere,* ★*goose,* ★*Goose,* ★*I'll,* ★*laugh,* ★*laughed,* ★*loose,* ★*rain,* ★*Rain,* ★*raindrops,* ★*Raindrops,* ★*rained,* ★*raining,* ★*Raining,* ★*rainy,* ★*woman*

Review • *a, A, another, Another, any, are, as, As, because, been, come, Come, could, do, Do, earth, egg, even, everyone, Everyone, fiction, from, From, gone, has, have, I, into, is, Is, isn't, I've, little, many, more, Mother, none, of, one, One, people, People, said, someone, something, the, The, their, there, There, They, to, today, two, very, was, wasn't, water, were, welcome, What, What's, where, Where, who, Who, you, You, your, zebras*

Comprehension

Comprehension Strategies

Priming Background Knowledge, Making Connections, Predicting, Identifying, Describing, Defining, Explaining, Inferring, Classifying, Visualizing, Summarizing, Sequencing, Monitoring Comprehension, Locating Information, Evaluating

Story Elements

Title, Who (Character), Where (Setting), When, Want (Goal), Problem, What (Action)

Story Vocabulary

★Cloud, ★Rain, ★Shower, ★Storm

Text Structure

Beginning, Middle, End

Expository Elements

Topic

Genre

Nonfiction • Narrative

Fiction • Narrative

Poem

Lesson

★Facts are sometimes stranger than fiction.

Written Response

Sentence Tracing, Sentence Illustration, Sentence Completion, Sentence Writing, Sentence Comprehension—Multiple Choice, Summarizing—Story Map, Conventions—Beginning Capital, Period

Fluency

Accuracy, Expression, Phrasing, Rate

Daily Lesson Planning

PACING

Some students will begin the process of learning to read slowly but make rapid progress later. If students complete Unit 38 by the end of the year, they will be at or above a beginning second grade reading level. Groups that are working at a slower pace may require more intensive *Read Well* instruction and practice. (See *Getting Started: A Guide to Implementation.*)

WEAK PASS CAUTION

If a student or students receive a Weak Pass on the previous two units, do not simply continue forward. See "Making Decisions" for Intervention Options.

ASSESSMENT

Upon completion of this unit, assess each student and proceed to Unit 37 as appropriate.

SAMPLE LESSON PLANS

The sample lesson plans illustrate how materials can be used for students with different learning needs. Each lesson plan is designed to provide daily decoding practice and story reading.

3-DAY PLAN		
Day 1	**Day 2**	**Day 3**
• Decoding Practice 1 • Introduction and Stories 1 and 2 • Comprehension Work 1b* • Comprehension Work 2* • Homework 1, Stories 1 and 2*	• Decoding Practice 2 • Stories 3 and 4 • Comprehension Work 3* • Comprehension Work 4* • Homework 2, Story 4*	• Decoding Practice 3 • Story 5, Summary, and Story 6 • Comprehension Work 5a* • Comprehension Work 6* • Homework 3, Story 5* • Homework 4, Story 6*

Note: To avoid excessive seatwork, 3- and 4-Day Plans omit or adjust use of Skill Work. If appropriate, Skill Work 1a and 5b can be used anytime during or after this unit as independent work or homework.

4-DAY PLAN			
Day 1	**Day 2**	**Day 3**	**Day 4**
• Decoding Practice 1 • Introduction and Stories 1 and 2 • Comprehension Work 1b* • Comprehension Work 2* • Homework 1, Stories 1 and 2*	• Decoding Practice 2 • Story 3 • Review Stories 1, 2, and 3 • Comprehension Work 3*	• Decoding Practice 3 • Stories 4 and 5, and Summary • Comprehension Work 4* • Comprehension Work 5a* • Homework 2, Story 4* • Homework 3, Story 5*	• Decoding Practice 4 • Story 6 • Review Solo Stories • Comprehension Work 6* • Skill Work 5b* • Homework 4, Story 6*

* From *Read Well* Comprehension and Skill Work (workbook), *Read Well* Homework (blackline masters), or Extra Practice in this book.

6-DAY PLAN		
Day 1 • Decoding Practice 1 • Introduction and Story 1 • Skill Work 1a* (Optional) • Comprehension Work 1b*	**Day 2** • Review Decoding Practice 1 • Story 2 • Comprehension Work 2* • Homework 1, Stories 1 and 2*	**Day 3** • Decoding Practice 2 • Story 3 • Comprehension Work 3*
Day 4 • Review Decoding Practice 2 • Story 4 • Comprehension Work 4* • Homework 2, Story 4*	**Day 5** • Decoding Practice 3 • Story 5 and Summary • Comprehension Work 5a* • Skill Work 5b* (Optional) • Homework 3, Story 5*	**Day 6** • Decoding Practice 4 • Story 6 • Comprehension Work 6* • Homework 4, Story 6*

PRE-INTERVENTION AND INTERVENTION

See *Getting Started: A Guide to Implementation* for information on how to achieve mastery at a faster pace with students who require eight or more days of instruction.

Note: Due to the sophistication of the latter units, many groups will benefit from the 6-Day Plan.

8-DAY PLAN • *Pre-Intervention*			
Day 1 • Decoding Practice 1 • Story 1 • Skill Work 1a* (Optional) • Comprehension Work 1b*	**Day 2** • Review Decoding Practice 1 • Story 2 • Comprehension Work 2* • Homework 1, Stories 1 and 2*	**Day 3** • Decoding Practice 2 • Story 3 • Comprehension Work 3*	**Day 4** • Review Decoding Practice 2 • Story 4 • Comprehension Work 4* • Homework 2, Story 4*
Day 5 • Decoding Practice 3 • Story 5 and Summary • Comprehension Work 5a* • Skill Work 5b* (Optional) • Homework 3, Story 5*	**Day 6** • Decoding Practice 4 • Story 6 • Comprehension Work 6* • Homework 4, Story 6*	**Day 7** • Extra Practice 1* • Extra Practice 1 Fluency Passage*	**Day 8** • Extra Practice 2* • Extra Practice 2 Fluency Passages*

10-DAY PLAN • *Intervention*				
Day 1 • Decoding Practice 1 • Story 1 • Skill Work 1a* (Optional) • Comprehension Work 1b*	**Day 2** • Review Decoding Practice 1 • Story 2 • Comprehension Work 2* • Homework 1, Stories 1 and 2*	**Day 3** • Decoding Practice 2 • Story 3 • Comprehension Work 3*	**Day 4** • Review Decoding Practice 2 • Story 4 • Comprehension Work 4* • Homework 2, Story 4*	**Day 5** • Decoding Practice 3 • Story 5 and Summary • Comprehension Work 5a* • Skill Work 5b* (Optional) • Homework 3, Story 5*
Day 6 • Decoding Practice 4 • Story 6 • Comprehension Work 6* • Homework 4, Story 6*	**Day 7** • Extra Practice 1* • Extra Practice 1 Fluency Passage*	**Day 8** • Extra Practice 2* • Extra Practice 2 Fluency Passages*	**Day 9** • Extra Practice 3* • Extra Practice 3 Fluency Passage*	**Day 10** • Extra Practice 4* • Extra Practice 4 Fluency Passage*

Materials and Materials Preparation

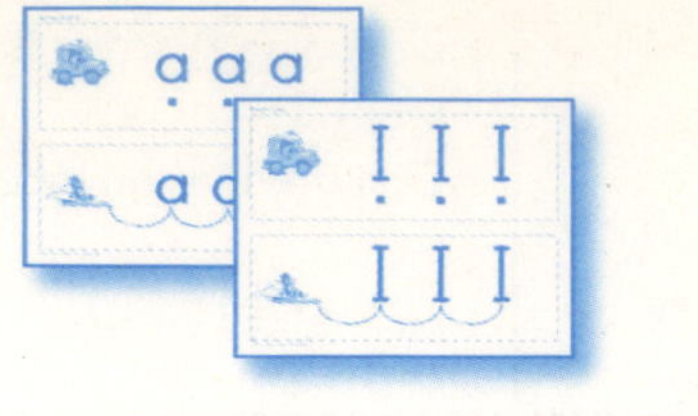

Core Lessons

Teacher Materials

***READ WELL* MATERIALS**

- Unit 36 Teacher's Guide
- Sound and Word Cards for Units 1–36
- Game markers (optional for use with cover-up activities)
- *Assessment Manual* or page 54

SCHOOL SUPPLIES

- Stopwatch or watch with a second hand

Student Materials

***READ WELL* MATERIALS**

- Decoding Book 4 for each student
- Unit 36 Storybook for each student
- Unit 36 Comprehension and Skill Work for each student (My Activity Book 4)
- Unit 36 Certificate of Achievement (blackline master page 55)
- Unit 36 Homework for each student (blackline masters) See *Getting Started* for suggested homework routines.

SCHOOL SUPPLIES

- Pencils, colors (optional—markers, crayons, or colored pencils)

Make one copy per student of each blackline master as appropriate for the group.

Note: For new or difficult Comprehension and Skill Work activities, make overhead transparencies from the blackline masters. Use the transparencies to demonstrate and guide practice.

Extra Practice Lessons

Note: Use these lessons only if needed.

Student Materials

***READ WELL* MATERIALS**

- Unit 36 Extra Practice 1 and 2 for each student (blackline master pages 59 and 63)
- Unit 36 Extra Practice 1, 2, 3, and 4 Fluency Passages for each student (blackline master pages 60, 64, 66, 68)
- Take-Home Game (blackline master page 61)

SCHOOL SUPPLIES

- Pencils, colors (markers, crayons, or colored pencils)
- White boards or paper

Important Tips

In this section, you will find:

★ Rapid Generalization of Skills

As students near completion of *Read Well 1*, growth is exponential. Review the skills students have learned.

Basic Comprehension Questions, Inferences, and High-Frequency Words

An additional focus on vocabulary and language skills often benefits English Language Learners and students with language delays.

In this sample lesson, continue assessing and building students' ability to answer basic comprehension questions. Add work on inferences as appropriate.

A list of oral language patterns used with high-frequency words is also provided for additional emphasis and practice across settings.

★Rapid Generalization of Skills

EXPONENTIAL GROWTH

After passing Unit 34, students have completed a basic phonetic sequence:

- All consonants: b, c, d, f, g, h, j, k, l, m, n, p, qu, r, s, t, v, w, x, y, z
- Single-letter vowels: a (short, schwa), e (long and short), i (short), o (long and short), u (short), -y (/ī/, /ē/)
- Consonant digraphs: th (voiced), th (unvoiced), sh, wh, ch
- Consonant blends: -nd, -nt, sw-, -st, sc-, thr-, tr-, sm-, cr, st-, -ct, dr-, sn-, -sk, kr, sl-, scr-, cl-, tw-, -str-, sk-, bl-, gr-, -ng, br-, fr-, fl-, gl-, pl-, spr-, sp-, spl-, pr-, -pt, wr-
- Vowel combinations: ee, ea, oo (long), oo (short), ay
- Silent e rule: a_e
- R-controls: ar, er, or
- Irregular word families: ank, all, other, old

In Units 35 through Unit 38, students add high-frequency vowel sounds to their repertoire:

- Silent e rule: i_e, o_e
- Vowel combinations: ou, ow (as in "cow"), ai, igh
- R-control: ir

SOUNDING OUT

By mastering the sounding out process in early lessons and increasing depth of knowledge in letter/sound recognition, *Read Well* students experience a rapid acceleration of skills and abilities as they progress through the final units of *Read Well 1*. The scope of their knowledge is evident in the number of new words they can read with ease.

End of Unit	New Words	Total Words
21	33	347
22	44	391
23	46	437
24	51	488
25	49	537
26	43	580
27	61	641
28	48	689
29	77	766
30	87	853
31	78	931
32	65	996
33	72	1068
34	95	1163
35	88	1251
36	109	1360
37	105	1465
38	152	1617

CAUTION

With students' advancing sophistication, it is easy to assume they can read anything. While this is often true of natural readers, other children require continual mastery-based instruction through the remaining high-frequency sounds and direct instruction in multisyllabic words.

In *Read Well Plus* Units 39 through 50, students add high-frequency vowel sounds to their repertoire:

- Consonant digraphs: ph, kn
- Letter combinations: aw, ew, u_e, ōw, ge, gi, ci, ce, oa, oi, ea, au, oy, dge

SECOND GRADE COMPLETION

Low-performing students sometimes require time during the summer or their second grade year to complete *Read Well 1*, Unit 38. For these students, we strongly recommend completing *Read Well 1*, Unit 38 *and Read Well Plus*. Because basal readers often include all vowels from early in a first grade program, *Read Well* students are best able to maintain their skills by using *Read Well Plus* as a bridge to a 2^2 basal reading program.

DEVELOPMENTALLY APPROPRIATE PRACTICE

Young children require different amounts of time and practice to master new skills. Mastery cannot be determined by the length of the school year. Schools are encouraged to continue with *Read Well* instruction in second grade with children who need the additional time to be successful. Every child deserves to read well.

Basic Comprehension Questions, Inferences, and High-Frequency Words

PREPARATION

Write your own sentences or use short, decodable sentences from the storybook. Act them out as appropriate.

◆◆ FOR ENGLISH LANGUAGE LEARNERS AND CHILDREN WITH LANGUAGE DELAYS

PROCEDURE

Have students read simple decodable sentences. As students demonstrate competency, encourage them to use complete sentences and make inferences.

The frog was sad because he had a sore leg.

Who is the sentence about? (The sentence is about the frog.)
What was the frog's problem? (He had a sore leg.)
Do you think the frog could hop? (No) *Why* not? (He had a sore leg.)
Why do you think the frog was sad? (He had a sore leg, and he couldn't hop.)

Have students help you compose simple sentences. Use question words to prompt what is written. (Non-decodable sentences can be read to students.) Say something like:

We're going to write a sentence about a frog. I'm going to write "The frog."
What should we have the frog do? ([Hop])
So, I'll add "[hopped]." What does our sentence say? (The frog [hopped].)
When do you want the frog [to hop]? ([Late one day])
So, I'll add "[Late one day]." Read the sentence. ([Late one day], the frog [hopped].)
Where do you want the frog to go? (To school)
Read the sentence. Late one day, the frog hopped to school.
Why do you think he went to school? ([To learn how to read])

ORAL LANGUAGE PATTERNS USED WITH NEW HIGH-FREQUENCY WORDS

Sentences for new high-frequency words are repeated below for additional language practice.

ORAL LANGUAGE PATTERNS ★High-Frequency Words Introduced in This Unit
★ out – I came in. He went . . . *out.*
★ around – We walked *around* the block.
★ down – The opposite of up is . . . *down.*
★ town – Let's go to . . . *town.*
★ Woman – Another word for a grown-up girl is a . . . *woman.*
★ again – Please [read the Tricky Words] . . . *again.*
★ now – We were late, so Mom said, "We need to go . . . *now.*"
★ How – *How* old are you?
★ found – I lost my hat, but then I . . . *found* it.
★ take – You can *take* a nap now.
★ don't – Another way to say "We do not [run in the halls]" is "We . . . *don't* [run in the halls]."

How to Teach the Lessons

Teach from this section. Each instructional component is outlined in an easy-to-teach format. Special tips are provided to help you nurture student progress.

Decoding Practice 1

- Storybook Introduction
- Story 1, Solo
- Skill Work Activity 1a
- Comprehension Work Activity 1b
- Story 2, Solo
- Comprehension Work Activity 2

Decoding Practice 2

- Story 3, Solo
- Comprehension Work Activity 3
- Story 4, Solo
- Comprehension Work Activity 4

Decoding Practice 3

- Story 5, Solo
- Story Summary
- Comprehension Work Activity 5a
- Skill Work Activity 5b
- Story 6, Solo
- Comprehension Work Activity 6

Decoding Practice 4

Review Solo Stories

BUILDING INDEPENDENCE

Next Steps • Principles of Instruction

For Units 21–38, follow the scaffolded principles of instruction below.

Provide demonstration and/or guided practice only with:
- New sounds
- Pattern words with new sounds
- New Tricky Words
- New multisyllabic words

Provide independent practice (practice without your assistance or voice) on:
- New and review pattern words with known sounds
- Review Tricky Words
- Review multisyllabic words

If students make errors, provide appropriate corrections.
- Have students identify any difficult sound and then sound out the word. Provide discrimination practice.
- Reintroduce difficult Tricky Words based on the initial introduction procedures.

If students require your assistance on words with known sounds, evaluate placement and consider a Jell-Well Review.

1 SOUND REVIEW

Note: Rotate easy cards in and out of practice.

> ◆◆ **FOR ENGLISH LANGUAGE LEARNERS AND CHILDREN WITH LANGUAGE DELAYS**
>
> Throughout Decoding Practice and Extra Practice, provide repeated use of the language patterns—both within and outside of lessons. See page 10 for tips.

2 NEW SOUND INTRODUCTION

★ **New sound: /ou/ as in "cloud"**

- Introduce the new sound /ou/ as in "cloud."
  Say something like:
  The letters ou say /ou/ as in "cloud." Tell me the sound. (/ou/)
  Look at the Heart Rows. All the words have your new sound . . . (/ou/).
  Say any underlined sound and then read the whole word.
- Provide repeated practice. Mix group and individual turns, independent of your voice.

3 NEW SOUND INTRODUCTION

★ **New sound: /ow/ as in "cow"**

- Introduce the new sound /ow/ as in "cow." Say something like:
  There are two spellings for the sound /ou/—o-u as in "cloud" and o-w as in "cow."
  Look at the Square Row. All the words have your new sound, /ow/, spelled with o-w.
  Tell me the sound. (/ow/)
  Say any underlined sound and then read the whole word.
- Provide repeated practice. Mix group and individual turns, independent of your voice.

4 ACCURACY AND FLUENCY BUILDING

- Have students say any underlined part, read the word, and practice the column.
- Provide repeated practice. Mix group and individual turns, independent of your voice.

5 MULTISYLLABIC WORDS

- Have students sound out each word to themselves and then read the word.
- Provide repeated practice. Mix group and individual turns, independent of your voice.

6 TRICKY WORDS

New Tricky Words: "Rain," "woman," "English," "Again"

★ For the Tricky Word "Rain," help students determine what says /ai/.
  Look at the first Tricky Word. It says "Rain." "Rain" isn't really tricky. It has a pattern that you haven't learned yet. Stretch out the word "Rain." /Rrrainnn/
  What sound do the letters a-i make? /ai/

- For the remaining words, have students read the word to themselves, then say the word following the appropriate sentence prompt below.
  A word for a grown-up girl is . . . *woman.* Mrs. [Shinn] is a . . . woman.
  People born in the United States are American. People born in England are . . . *English.*
  Please read the Tricky Words . . . *again.*
- Have students read the row. Repeat, mixing group and individual turns, independent of your voice.

7 DAILY STORY READING

Proceed to the Unit 36 Storybook. See Daily Lesson Planning for pacing suggestions.

8 COMPREHENSION AND SKILL WORK ACTIVITY 1 AND/OR ACTIVITY 2

See pages 20, 21, and/or 25.

UNIT 36 DECODING PRACTICE 1 ✿
(For use with Stories 1 and 2)

1. SOUND REVIEW Use Sound Cards for Units 1–35.

★2. NEW SOUND INTRODUCTION Introduce /ou/ as in "cloud." For each word, have students say any underlined part, then read the word.

♥	★ ou	sound	clouds	ground
♥♥	out	shouted	about	around

★3. NEW SOUND INTRODUCTION Introduce /ow/ as in "cow." For each word, have students say any underlined part, then read the word.

■	★ ow	how	down	town	shower

4. ACCURACY/FLUENCY BUILDING For each column, have students say any underlined part, then read each word. Next, have students practice the column.

▲	●	✈
houses	however	lick
safety	indoors	leak
planet	everyone	luck
ever	everywhere	like

5. MULTISYLLABIC WORDS Have students silently figure out each word and read it aloud.

☆	summer	happening	expected

★6. TRICKY WORDS See the Teacher's Guide for how to introduce each word. Next, have students silently figure out each word and read it aloud.

✎	★Rain	★woman	★English	★Again

7. DAILY STORY READING

25

◆◆ SENTENCE SUGGESTIONS

Use gestures for "in" and "out," "around," "up," and "down."

♥♥ out – I came in. He went . . . *out.*

♥♥ around – We walked . . . *around* the block.

■ down – The opposite of up is . . . *down.*

■ town – Let's go to . . . *town.*

▲ ever – He said, "I won't *ever* tell a lie."

☆expected – We looked at the dark clouds and *expected* it to rain.

☆happening – She asked, "What's . . . *happening*?"

Sentence Suggestions: If a sentence is included, use it *after* decoding the individual word. The sentences may be used to build oral language patterns and vocabulary. Use of sentences also emphasizes that words have meaning.

1 INTRODUCING THE STORYBOOK AND THE TITLE PAGE

Identifying—Title, Priming Background Knowledge, Classifying

Vocabulary—Fact, Fiction

Ask students what they already know about the words "fact" and "fiction."

Say something like:

You already know that a fact is something . . . that is real.

In the last unit, you learned that fiction is something that is . . . made up.

Your new book is called *Fact or Fiction*.

What kind of story was "The Case of the Missing Ring," fact or fiction? (Fiction)

How could you tell?

What kind of story was "A Dry Desert Home," fact or fiction? (Fact)

Predicting

Unit 36 is "Weather Tales."

What kinds of stories do you think are in this unit?

2 INTRODUCING VOCABULARY

Vocabulary—Cloud, Rain, Shower, Storm

Cloud

Put your finger under the first picture.

★ What do you already know about a cloud?

This is a definition for a cloud.

A *cloud* is something that floats high in the sky. A cloud is made up of tiny drops of water.

Clouds are an important part of this story.

Rain

Put your finger under the next picture.

What do you already know about rain?

This is a definition for rain.

Rain is water that falls in drops from the clouds.

Shower

Put your finger under the next picture.

A *shower* is a short fall of rain. In a shower, it doesn't rain very long.

Storm

Put your finger under the next picture.

A *storm* is a strong wind with rain, ice, or snow.

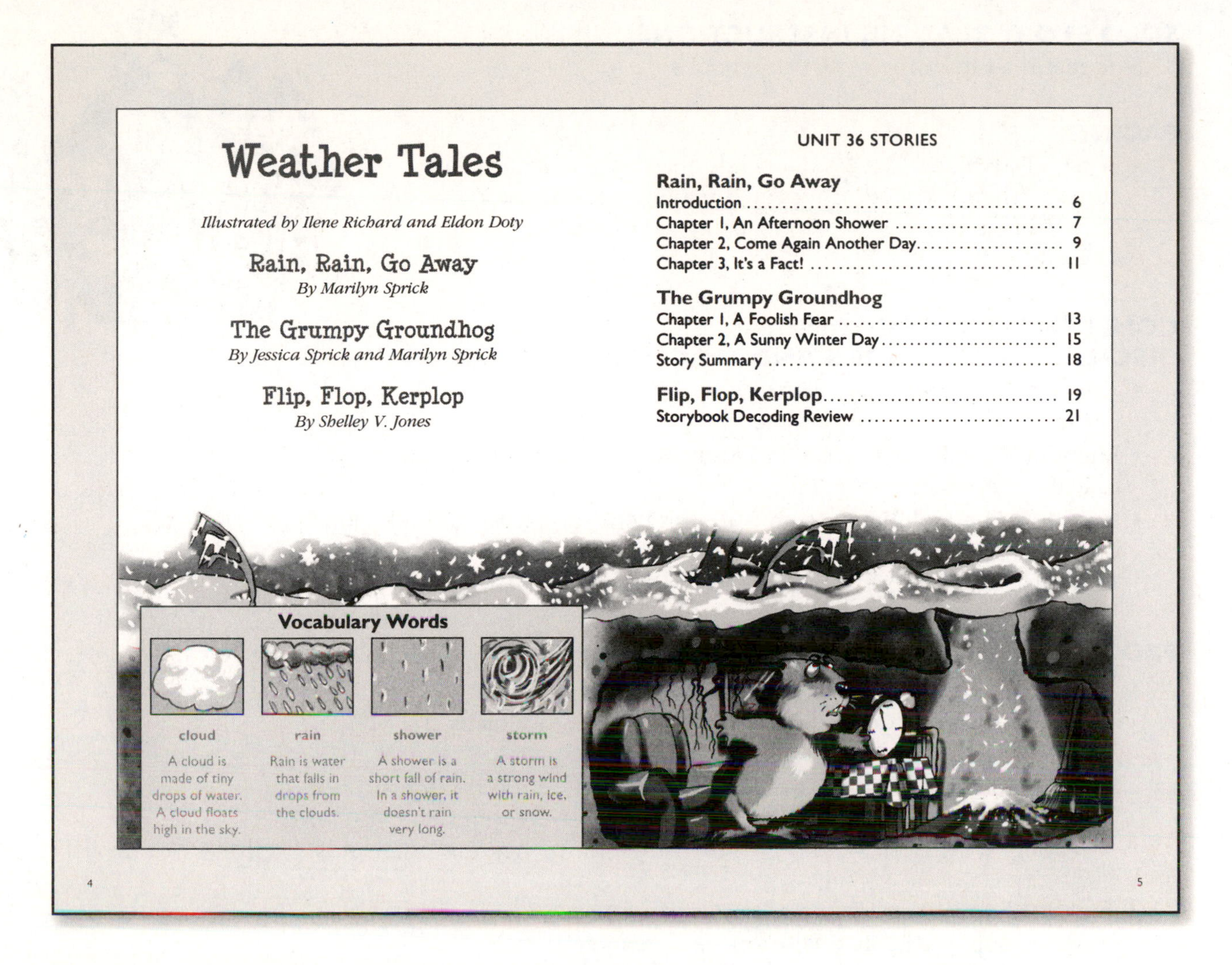

Weather Tales

Illustrated by Ilene Richard and Eldon Doty

Rain, Rain, Go Away
By Marilyn Sprick

The Grumpy Groundhog
By Jessica Sprick and Marilyn Sprick

Flip, Flop, Kerplop
By Shelley V. Jones

UNIT 36 STORIES

Vocabulary Words

cloud — A cloud is made of tiny drops of water. A cloud floats high in the sky.

rain — Rain is water that falls in drops from the clouds.

shower — A shower is a short fall of rain. In a shower, it doesn't rain very long.

storm — A storm is a strong wind with rain, ice, or snow.

4 5

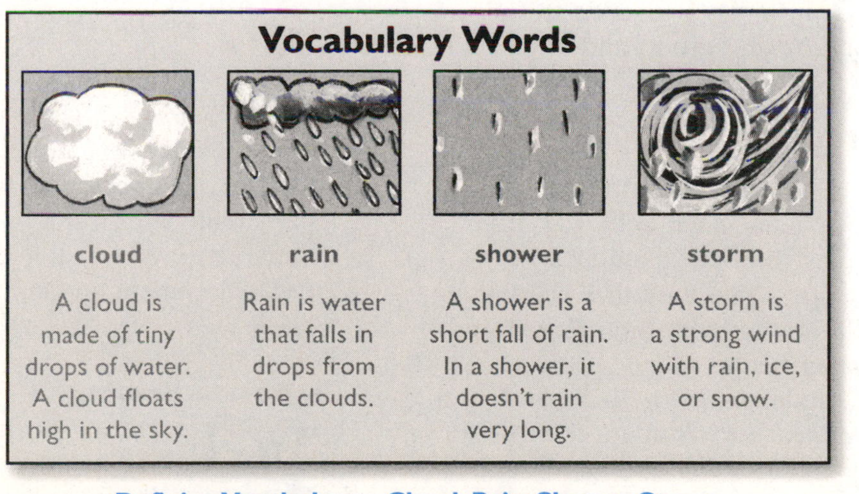

Vocabulary Words

cloud — A cloud is made of tiny drops of water. A cloud floats high in the sky.

rain — Rain is water that falls in drops from the clouds.

shower — A shower is a short fall of rain. In a shower, it doesn't rain very long.

storm — A storm is a strong wind with rain, ice, or snow.

Defining Vocabulary—Cloud, Rain, Shower, Storm

SOLO STORY READING INSTRUCTIONS

Students read from their own storybooks.

PACING

- 3- to 4-Day Plans: Have students do the first reading of Solo Story 1. Then proceed to repeated readings of Solo Story 2.
- 6- to 10-Day Plans: Have students do the first *and* second readings.

COMPREHENSION BUILDING: DISCUSSION QUESTIONS AND TEACHER THINK ALOUDS

- Ask questions and discuss text on the *second* reading when indicated in the storybook in light gray text.
- Encourage students to answer questions with complete sentences and to elaborate when appropriate.
- If students have difficulty with a comprehension question, think aloud with them or reread the portion of the story that answers the question. Then, ask the question again.

PROCEDURES

1. First Reading

- Have students individually whisper read the story using their fingers to track text.
- After students complete the first reading and before the second reading, have students practice a few paragraphs. First demonstrate expressive reading for students, then give individual turns. Acknowledge student efforts.

2. Second Reading

- Mix group and individual turns, independent of your voice. Have students work toward an accuracy goal of 0–2 errors. Quietly keep track of errors made by all students in each group.
- After reading the story, practice any difficult words.
- If the group has not reached the accuracy goal, have the group reread the story, mixing group and individual turns.

3. Repeated Readings

a. Timed Readings

- Once the accuracy goal has been achieved, have individual students read the page while the other children track the text with their fingers and whisper read. Time individuals for 30 seconds and encourage each student to work for a personal best.
- Count the number of words read correctly in 30 seconds (words read minus errors). Multiply by two to determine words correct per minute. Record student scores.

Note: If a student is unable to read with close to 100% accuracy, the personal goal should be accuracy. If the student is unable to read with accuracy, evaluate group placement and consider a Jell-Well Review.

b. Partner Reading

During students' daily independent work, have them do Partner Reading.

STORY 1, SOLO

fiction = something that is made up
fact = something that is real

FINGER TRACKING
(Reminder)
Continue having children track the large text with their fingers.

Rain, Rain, Go Away

Introduction

When someone makes up a story, the story is called fiction. The stories about the detectives, Zack and Alexander, were fiction. Bats do not have hats. Raccoons do not have wedding rings, and zebras are not detectives.

When you read this next story, it may be hard to tell whether it is fact or fiction.

6

STORY 1, SOLO

CHAPTER 1

An Afternoon Shower

When does this story take place?[1] The chapter is called "An Afternoon Shower." A shower is a light rain.[2] So what do you think this story is about?[3]

One summer day in a small English town, clouds began to darken the sky. It had been a dry summer. The people looked up at the clouds and said, "The rain will be welcome!"

Why were the people looking forward to the rain?[4]

7

1. **Identifying—When** (The story takes place in the afternoon.)
2. **Teacher Think Aloud, Using Vocabulary—Shower**
3. **Inferring** (The story is about a light rain in the afternoon.)
4. **Inferring, Explaining** (The people were looking forward to the rain because it had been a dry summer.)

The people expected an afternoon shower. However, when the rain started to fall, it was more than just a shower.

The people could hear funny sounds all around them. Whack! Plop, plop, plop! Plop, plop, whack! Everyone ran indoors.

Where did the people run?[1] Why do you think they ran indoors?[2]

FOCUS ON VOCABULARY, VISUALIZING, CLASSIFYING

After completing the page, say something like: Close your eyes. Imagine there is an afternoon shower.

Now imagine that you hear funny sounds all around you. Listen. "Whack! Plop, plop, plop! Plop, plop, whack!"

You run indoors. Could this be something that really happened to people? (Yes)

Could this be fact? Could it be fiction? At this point, the story could be fact *or* fiction.

1. **Identifying—Where** (The people ran indoors.)
2. **Inferring** (The people ran to get out of the rain.)

SOUND PAGE

Use work pages from the workbook.

UNIT 36 SKILL WORK ACTIVITY 1a
For use after Story 1

Name ____________________

ow ou

ow cow down brown

ou our out about

round around town

61

CHECKOUT OPPORTUNITY

While students are working on Comprehension and Skill Work, you may wish to listen to individuals read a Decoding Practice or Solo Story. If the student makes an error, gently correct and have the student reread the column, row, or sentence.

PROCEDURES

For each step, demonstrate and guide practice as needed.

1. Handwriting—Basic Instructions

- Have students identify the letter combinations ow and ou.
- Have students trace the letter combinations and the words—leaving a finger space between each combination or word.
- In each row have students circle their best word.

2. Drawing Pictures That Use /ow/ and /ou/—Basic Instructions

- Have students fill the box with things that use /ow/ and /ou/. Students can write the letters ow and ou, draw pictures of things that use /ow/ and /ou/, cut out and paste on pictures of things that use /ow/ and /ou/, or cut out and paste on words that use /ow/ and /ou/.

Note: Neat work helps students take pride in their efforts. Periodically, comment on students' progress and best efforts.

STORY COMPREHENSION

Use work pages from the workbook.

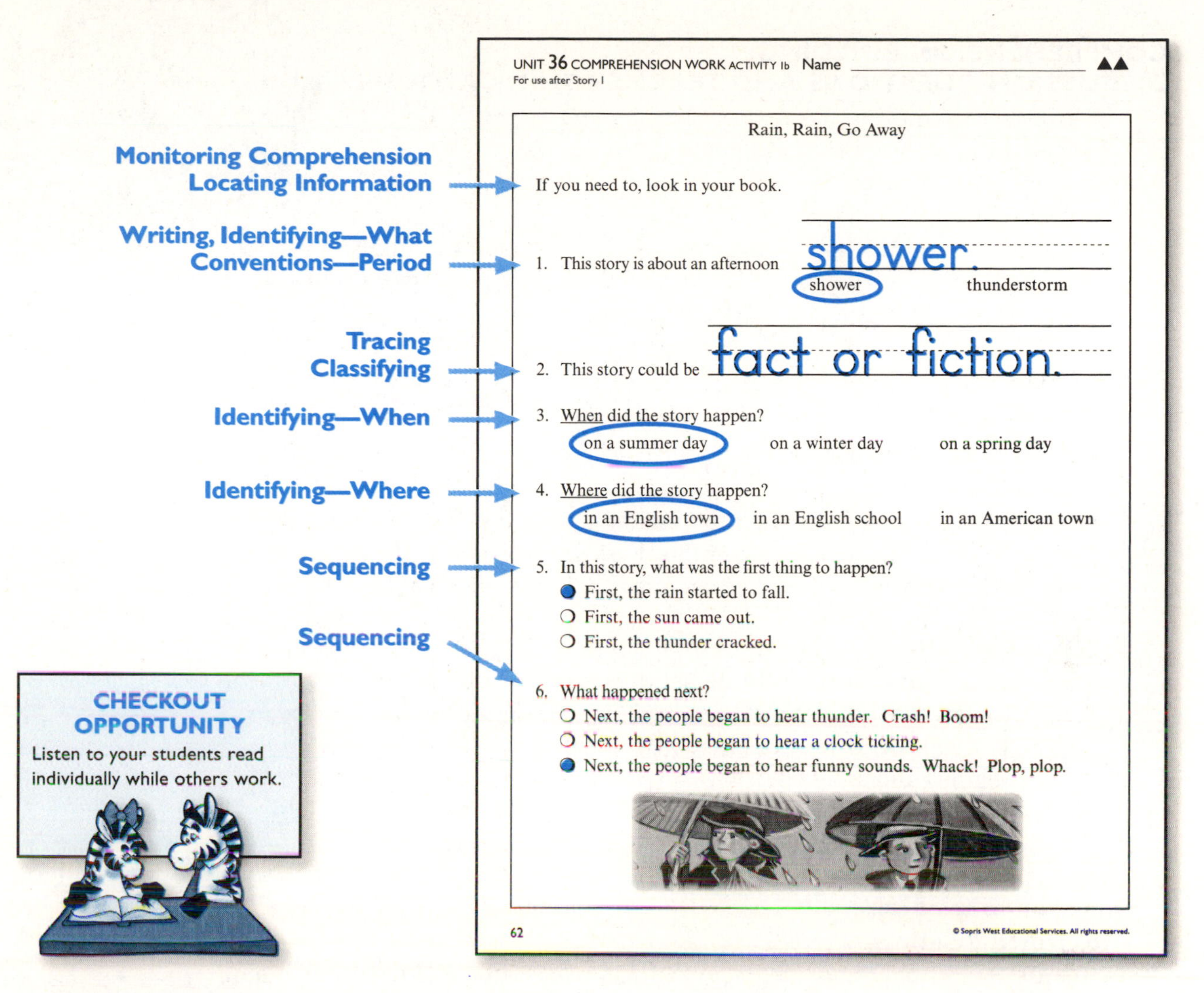

UNIT 36 COMPREHENSION WORK ACTIVITY 1b Name ______________ ▲▲
For use after Story 1

Rain, Rain, Go Away

If you need to, look in your book.

1. This story is about an afternoon shower.
   (shower) thunderstorm

2. This story could be fact or fiction.

3. When did the story happen?
   (on a summer day) on a winter day on a spring day

4. Where did the story happen?
   (in an English town) in an English school in an American town

5. In this story, what was the first thing to happen?
   - ● First, the rain started to fall.
   - ○ First, the sun came out.
   - ○ First, the thunder cracked.

6. What happened next?
   - ○ Next, the people began to hear thunder. Crash! Boom!
   - ○ Next, the people began to hear a clock ticking.
   - ● Next, the people began to hear funny sounds. Whack! Plop, plop.

62

PROCEDURES

For each step, demonstrate and guide practice as needed.

- (Demonstrate) Have students orally respond to items while you demonstrate how to complete the page.
- (Guide) Have students orally respond to the items, but do not demonstrate how to complete the page.
- (Independent With Support) Have students silently read over the items and ask any questions they may have.

1. Multiple Choice, Sentence Completion—Basic Instructions (Item 1)
- Have students select and circle the word that correctly completes the sentence.
- Have them write the answer in the blank and place a period at the end.

2. Sentence Completion—Basic Instructions (Item 2)

Have students read, complete the sentence, and end the sentence with a period.

3. Multiple Choice—Basic Instructions (Items 3, 4, 5, 6)

Have students circle the words or fill in the bubble for the correct answer. Periodically, think aloud with students. Discuss the multiple choice options. As appropriate, ask questions like: "Does the first answer make sense?" "Is that what the book said?" "Is the answer completely correct?"

SOLO STORY READING INSTRUCTIONS

Students read from their own storybooks.

COMPREHENSION BUILDING: DISCUSSION QUESTIONS AND TEACHER THINK ALOUDS

- Ask questions and discuss text on the *second* reading when indicated in the storybook in light gray text.
- Encourage students to answer questions with complete sentences and to elaborate when appropriate.
- If students have difficulty with a comprehension question, think aloud with them or reread the portion of the story that answers the question. Then, ask the question again.

PROCEDURES

1. First Reading

- Have students individually whisper read the story, using their fingers to track text.
- After students complete the first reading and before the second reading, have students practice a paragraph. First demonstrate expressive reading for students, then give individual turns. Acknowledge student efforts.

2. Second Reading

- Mix group and individual turns, independent of your voice. Have students work toward an accuracy goal of 0–2 errors. Quietly keep track of errors made by all students in each group.
- After reading the story, practice any difficult words.
- If the group has not reached the accuracy goal, have the group reread the story, mixing group and individual turns.

3. Repeated Readings

a. Timed Readings

- Once the accuracy goal has been achieved, have individual students read the page while the other children track the text with their fingers and whisper read.

  Time individuals for 30 seconds and encourage each student to work for a personal best.
- Count the number of words read correctly in 30 seconds (words read minus errors). Multiply by two to determine words correct per minute. Record student scores.

b. Partner Reading

During students' daily independent work, have them do Partner Reading.

c. Homework 1

Have students read the story at home. (A reprint of this story is available on a blackline master in *Read Well* Homework.)

STORY 2, SOLO

CHAPTER 2

Come Again Another Day

The people looked out at the rain from the safety of their houses. They started to see funny things in the rain. People asked, "What is happening?"

One man said, "It's raining cats and dogs!"

A woman said, "Maybe the sky is falling!"

It did look as if lumps of mud were falling from the sky.

Do you have any ideas about what might have been happening? **1**

Another man asked, "Do you think that rain could be from another planet?"

Just then, someone shouted, "That rain is green."

Then another woman shouted, "The rain is green and it is hopping!"

What did the people see? **2** What do you think could be green and hopping? **3**

9

FOCUS ON VOCABULARY, CLASSIFYING

After completing the page, say something like: *Have you ever seen green, hopping rain?*

Do you think this story is fact or fiction?

1 Inferring

2 Identifying—What (The people saw that the rain was green and hopping.)

3 Predicting

STORY 2, SOLO

It was raining frogs! Frogs were falling from the clouds. Hundreds of frogs landed in the trees, on the cars, and on the ground. There were frogs everywhere.

Have you ever seen frog rain?[1] Do you think this story is fact or fiction?[2] What is a fact?[3] Do you think the frog rain really happened?[4] If the story is real, it is . . .[5] If the story is made up, it is . . .[6]

10

1. **Making Connections**
2. **Evaluating, Classifying**
3. **Using Vocabulary—Fact** (A fact is something that is true.)
4. **Evaluating**
5. **Using Vocabulary—Fact** (fact)
6. **Using Vocabulary—Fiction** (fiction)

STORY COMPREHENSION

Use work pages from the workbook.

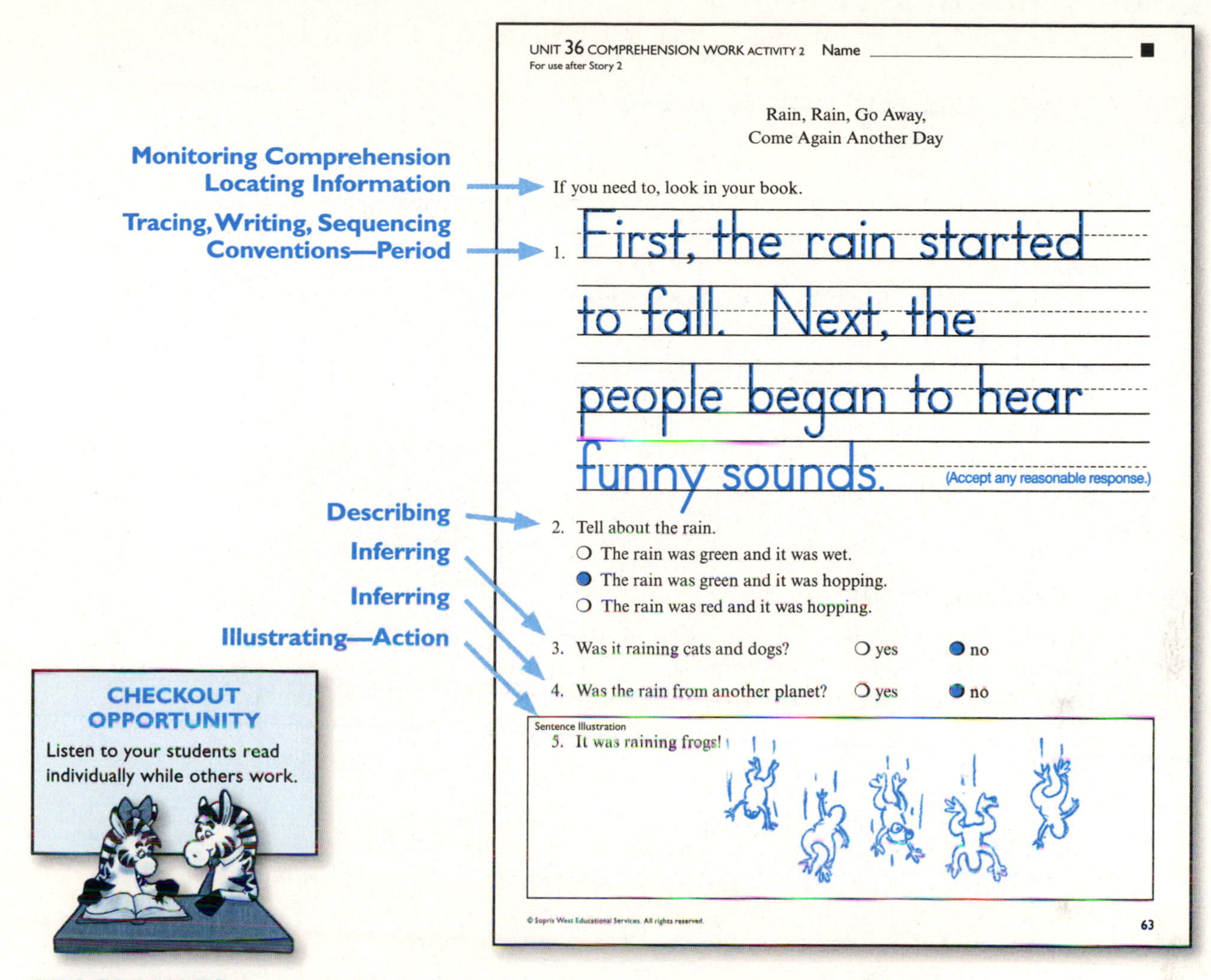

UNIT 36 COMPREHENSION WORK ACTIVITY 2 Name ______
For use after Story 2

Rain, Rain, Go Away,
Come Again Another Day

If you need to, look in your book.

1. First, the rain started to fall. Next, the people began to hear funny sounds. (Accept any reasonable response.)

2. Tell about the rain.
   - ○ The rain was green and it was wet.
   - ● The rain was green and it was hopping.
   - ○ The rain was red and it was hopping.

3. Was it raining cats and dogs? ○ yes ● no

4. Was the rain from another planet? ○ yes ● no

Sentence Illustration
5. It was raining frogs!

© Sopris West Educational Services. All rights reserved.

63

PROCEDURES

For each step, demonstrate and guide practice as needed.

1. Paragraph Completion—Basic Instructions (Item 1)
Have students read, trace, and complete the sentences. Remind them to end each sentence with a period.

2. Multiple Choice—Basic Instructions (Items 2, 3, 4)
Have students fill in the bubble for the correct answer. Periodically, think aloud with students. Discuss the multiple choice options. As appropriate, ask questions like: "Does the first answer make sense?" "Is that what the book said?" "Is the answer completely correct?"

3. Sentence Illustration—Basic Instructions (Item 5)
Have students read the sentence and then complete the illustration.

1 SOUND REVIEW

◆◆ 2 SOUNDING OUT SMOOTHLY

Provide repeated practice. Mix group and individual turns, independent of your voice.

◆◆ 3 ACCURACY AND FLUENCY BUILDING

Repeat practice on each column, building accuracy first and then fluency. Say something like:

Touch under the first word in the Heart Column. Read the underlined part. (happen)
Read the whole word. (happened) What . . . *happened?*
Next word. (suck)
Whole word. (sucked) The baby *sucked* her thumb.
Next word. (popp)
Whole word. (popped) Jack *popped* out of bed.
Read the whole column. (happened . . . sucked . . . popped)
Read the words a little faster. (happened, sucked, popped)
[Jason], first word. (happened)
[Jermaine], next word. (sucked)
[Natasha], next word. (popped)

4 MULTISYLLABIC WORDS

- Have students sound out each part, then read the whole word aloud. Use the words in sentences as needed.
- Provide repeated practice. Mix group and individual turns, independent of your voice.

◆◆ 5 TRICKY WORDS

★ **New Tricky Word: "laughed"**

- To introduce the new Tricky Word "laughed," say something like:

  Your new word is *really* tricky. Let's use the sounds we know and see if we can sound it out.
  /lllăăăŭŭŭghĕĕĕd/
  That's really goofy. The word is "laughed." Tell me the word. (laughed)
  It was funny so we . . . *laughed.*
- Have students read the rows. Repeat, mixing group and individual turns, independent of your voice.

6 DAILY STORY READING

Proceed to the Unit 36 Storybook. See Daily Lesson Planning for pacing suggestions.

7 COMPREHENSION AND SKILL WORK ACTIVITY 3 AND/OR ACTIVITY 4

See pages 31 and/or 35.

Note: The light scripting in *Read Well* will help you visualize instruction as you prepare for a lesson. Scripting provides an instructional guide and is not intended to be memorized or read to students.

◆◆ For ELLs and children with language delays, provide repeated and extended practice with the language patterns. See page 10 for tips.

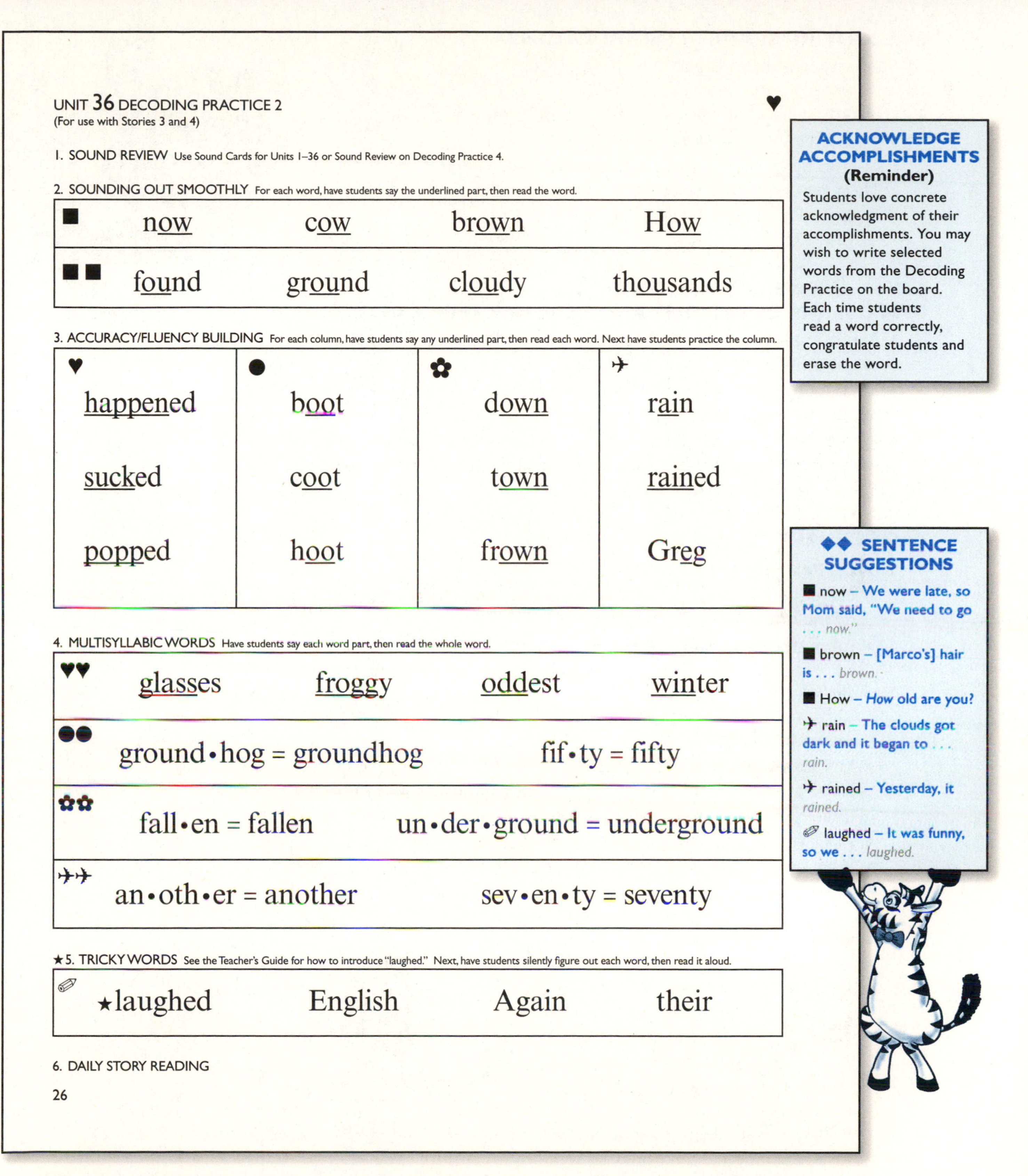

UNIT 36 DECODING PRACTICE 2 ♥
(For use with Stories 3 and 4)

1. SOUND REVIEW Use Sound Cards for Units 1–36 or Sound Review on Decoding Practice 4.

2. SOUNDING OUT SMOOTHLY For each word, have students say the underlined part, then read the word.

■	now	cow	brown	How
■■	found	ground	cloudy	thousands

3. ACCURACY/FLUENCY BUILDING For each column, have students say any underlined part, then read each word. Next have students practice the column.

♥	●	✿	✈
happened	boot	down	rain
sucked	coot	town	rained
popped	hoot	frown	Greg

4. MULTISYLLABIC WORDS Have students say each word part, then read the whole word.

♥♥	glasses	froggy	oddest	winter
●●	ground•hog = groundhog		fif•ty = fifty	
✿✿	fall•en = fallen		un•der•ground = underground	
✈✈	an•oth•er = another		sev•en•ty = seventy	

★5. TRICKY WORDS See the Teacher's Guide for how to introduce "laughed." Next, have students silently figure out each word, then read it aloud.

✏	★laughed	English	Again	their

6. DAILY STORY READING

26

ACKNOWLEDGE ACCOMPLISHMENTS (Reminder)

Students love concrete acknowledgment of their accomplishments. You may wish to write selected words from the Decoding Practice on the board. Each time students read a word correctly, congratulate students and erase the word.

◆◆ SENTENCE SUGGESTIONS

■ now – We were late, so Mom said, "We need to go . . . *now.*"

■ brown – [Marco's] hair is . . . *brown.*

■ How – *How old are you?*

✈ rain – The clouds got dark and it began to . . . *rain.*

✈ rained – Yesterday, it *rained.*

✏ laughed – It was funny, so we . . . *laughed.*

Sentence Suggestions: Use the appropriate suggested sentence *after* decoding each individual word.

SOLO STORY READING INSTRUCTIONS

Students read from their own storybooks.

PACING

- 3- to 4-Day Plans: Have students do the first reading of Solo Story 3.
  Then proceed to repeated readings of Solo Story 4.
- 6- to 10-Day Plans: Have students do the first *and* second readings.

COMPREHENSION BUILDING: DISCUSSION QUESTIONS AND TEACHER THINK ALOUDS

- Ask questions and discuss text on the *second* reading when indicated in the storybook in light gray text.
- Encourage students to answer questions with complete sentences and to elaborate when appropriate.
- If students have difficulty with a comprehension question, think aloud with them or reread the portion of the story that answers the question. Then, ask the question again.

PROCEDURES

1. First Reading

- Have students individually whisper read the story, using their fingers to track text.
- After students complete the first reading and before the second reading, have students practice a paragraph. First demonstrate expressive reading for students, then give individual turns. Acknowledge student efforts.

2. Second Reading

- Mix group and individual turns, independent of your voice.
  Have students work toward an accuracy goal of 0–2 errors.
  Quietly keep track of errors made by all students in each group.
- After reading the story, practice any difficult words.
- If the group has not reached the accuracy goal, have the group reread the story, mixing group and individual turns.

3. Repeated Readings

a. Timed Readings

- Once the accuracy goal has been achieved, have individual students read the page while the other children track the text with their fingers and whisper read.
  Time individuals for 30 seconds and encourage each student to work for a personal best.
- Determine words correct per minute. Record student scores.

b. Partner Reading

During students' daily independent work, have them do Partner Reading.

c. Homework 2

Have students read the story at home. (A reprint of this story is available on a blackline master in *Read Well* Homework.)

STORY 3, SOLO

CHAPTER 3

It's a Fact!

As odd as it may seem, it is a fact. Frogs have fallen from the clouds.

In "Come Again Another Day," you learned that frogs rained down on an English town. It happened about seventy years ago. Strong winds had sucked lots of little frogs up into the clouds. When the rain started, the frogs fell from the clouds with the rain. It really was a froggy day!

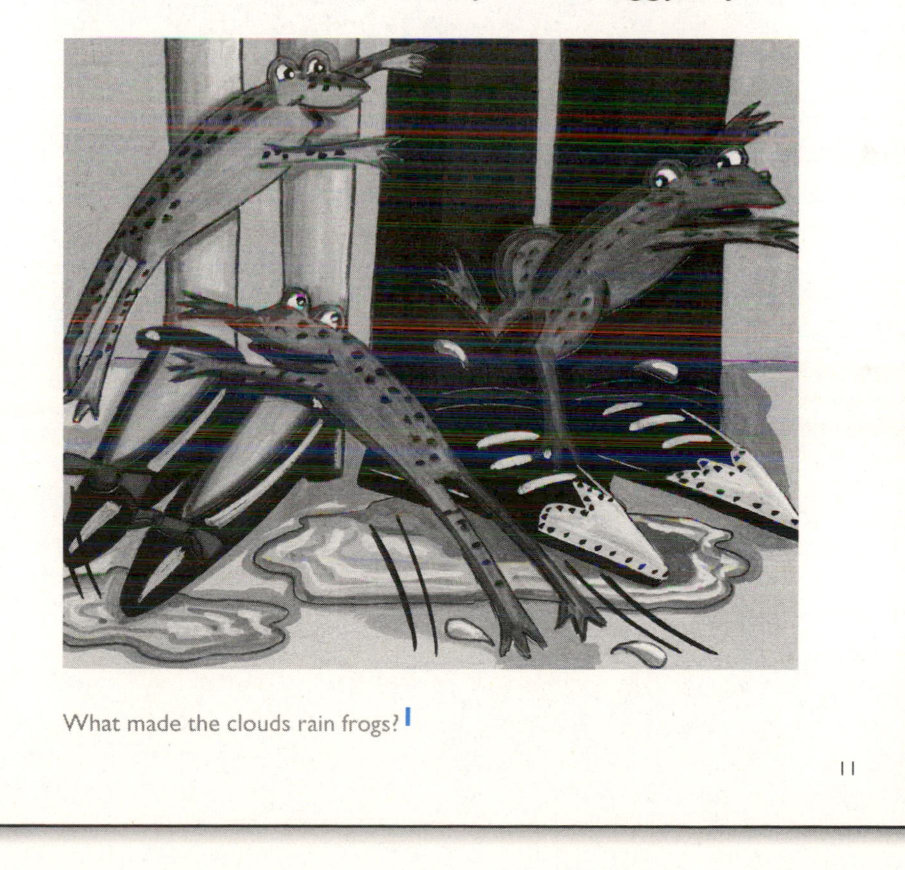

What made the clouds rain frogs? [1]

[1] **Explaining** (Strong winds had sucked the frogs up into the clouds. Then the frogs fell with the rain.)

STORY 3, SOLO

Frog rain isn't the oddest thing that has ever happened. About one hundred fifty years ago, thousands of fish fell into the streets of another town. No one ever found out where the fish came from. But the fish soon began to smell. Fish rain wasn't very funny for the people who had to clean it up!

You know why it rained frogs. Do you think you know why it rained fish?[1]

12

[1] **Inferring, Explaining** (A strong wind probably lifted the fish into the clouds. Then when it rained, the fish fell with the rain.)

STORY COMPREHENSION

Use work pages from the workbook.

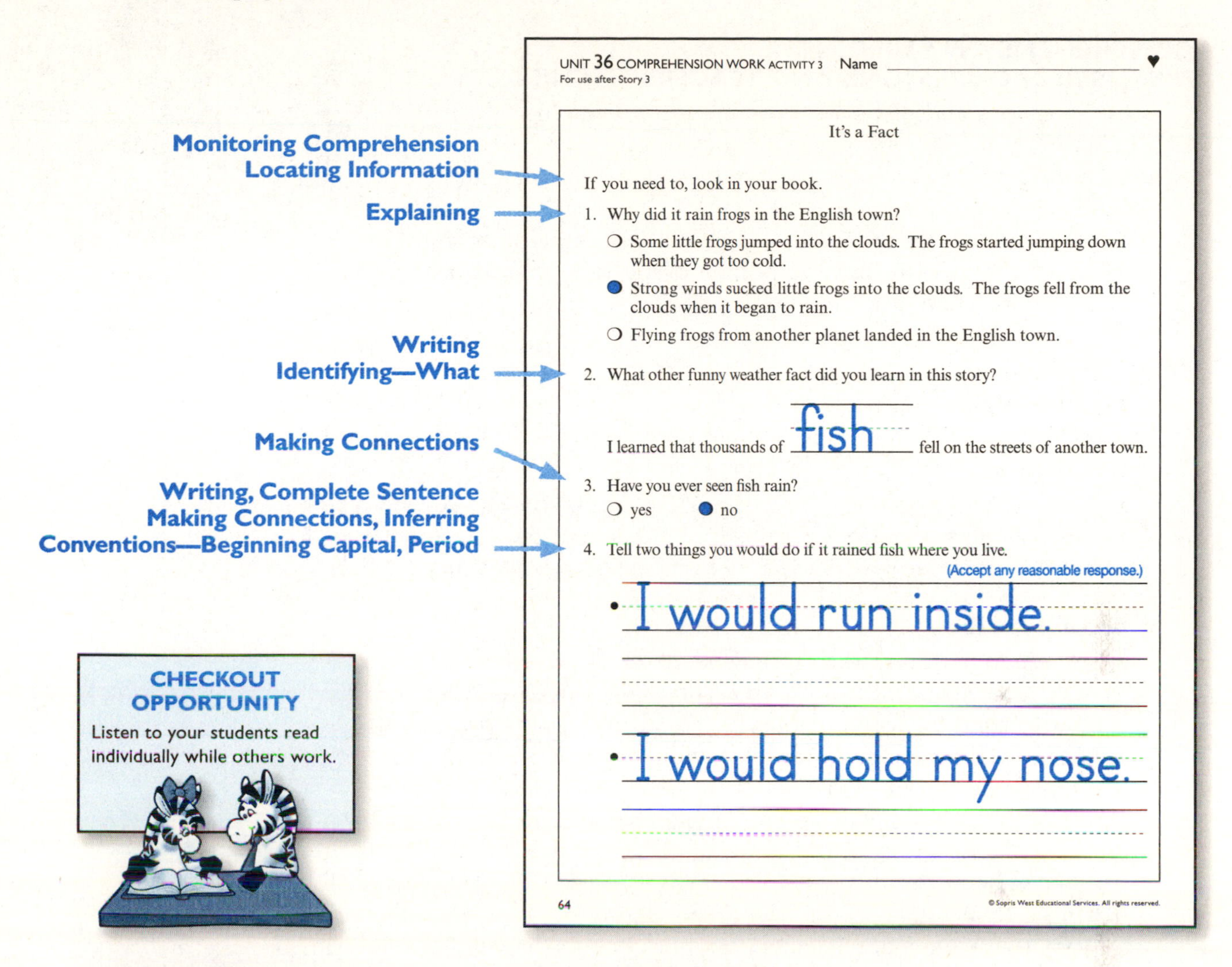

UNIT 36 COMPREHENSION WORK ACTIVITY 3 Name ________________
For use after Story 3

It's a Fact

If you need to, look in your book.

1. Why did it rain frogs in the English town?
   - ○ Some little frogs jumped into the clouds. The frogs started jumping down when they got too cold.
   - ● Strong winds sucked little frogs into the clouds. The frogs fell from the clouds when it began to rain.
   - ○ Flying frogs from another planet landed in the English town.

2. What other funny weather fact did you learn in this story?

   I learned that thousands of **fish** fell on the streets of another town.

3. Have you ever seen fish rain?
   ○ yes ● no

4. Tell two things you would do if it rained fish where you live.
   (Accept any reasonable response.)
   - I would run inside.
   - I would hold my nose.

64

© Sopris West Educational Services. All rights reserved.

PROCEDURES

For each step, demonstrate and guide practice as needed.

1. Multiple Choice—Basic Instructions (Items 1, 3)

Have students fill in the bubble for the correct answer. Periodically, think aloud with students. Discuss the multiple choice options. As appropriate, ask questions like: "Does the first answer make sense?" "Is that what the book said?" "Is the answer completely correct?"

2. Sentence Completion—Basic Instructions (Item 2)

Have students read and complete the sentence.

3. Sentence Writing—Basic Instructions (Item 4)

- Have students read the direction and brainstorm possible responses using complete sentences.
- Have students write complete sentences that start with a capital letter and end with a period.

SOLO STORY READING INSTRUCTIONS

Students read from their own storybooks.

COMPREHENSION BUILDING: DISCUSSION QUESTIONS AND TEACHER THINK ALOUDS

- Ask questions and discuss text on the *second* reading when indicated in the storybook in light gray text.
- Encourage students to answer questions with complete sentences and to elaborate when appropriate.
- If students have difficulty with a comprehension question, think aloud with them or reread the portion of the story that answers the question. Then, ask the question again.

PROCEDURES

1. First Reading

- Have students individually whisper read the story, using their fingers to track text.
- After students complete the first reading and before the second reading, have students practice a paragraph. First demonstrate expressive reading for students, then give individual turns. Acknowledge student efforts.

2. Second Reading

- Mix group and individual turns, independent of your voice. Have students work toward an accuracy goal of 0–2 errors. Quietly keep track of errors made by all students in each group.
- After reading the story, practice any difficult words.
- If the group has not reached the accuracy goal, have the group reread the story, mixing group and individual turns.

3. Repeated Readings

a. Timed Readings

- Once the accuracy goal has been achieved, have individual students read the page while the other children track the text with their fingers and whisper read.

  Time individuals for 30 seconds and encourage each student to work for a personal best.
- Count the number of words read correctly in 30 seconds (words read minus errors). Multiply by two to determine words correct per minute. Record student scores.

b. Partner Reading

During students' daily independent work, have them do Partner Reading.

c. Homework 2

Have students read the story at home. (A reprint of this story is available on a blackline master in *Read Well* Homework.)

STORY 4, SOLO

The Grumpy Groundhog

CHAPTER 1

A Foolish Fear

Some people say that groundhogs can predict weather. They say if a groundhog comes out of his hole on a sunny day in late winter and sees his shadow, he will go back into his tunnel and spring won't come.[1] Do you think groundhogs can really predict the weather?[2]

Your next story is about a groundhog named Greg. Greg has decided never to come out of his hole, so it is always winter.[3] Do you think this story is fact or fiction?[4]

Long ago, there was a grumpy old groundhog named Greg. Grumpy Greg lived in a dark, round tunnel and never came out. It was all because of a foolish fear—the big black thing he saw whenever he went out. So Greg stayed underground for years and years. Spring never came, and it was always cold.

What do you think Greg's foolish fear was?[5] Yes, given what we know about groundhog stories, Greg's foolish fear was his shadow.[6] Read the passage again.

Who is the story about?[7] Greg is causing a problem. What's the problem?[8] Is this story fact or fiction?[9]

13

1. **Teacher Think Aloud**
2. **Inferring**
3. **Teacher Think Aloud**
4. **Classifying**
5. **Inferring**
6. **Teacher Think Aloud**
7. **Identifying—Who, Describing** (The story is about a grumpy old groundhog named Greg.)
8. **Explaining** (It is always cold and spring never comes because Greg has a foolish fear and stays underground.)
9. **Classifying** (This story is fiction.)

STORY 4, SOLO

One day, a hip gray rabbit in dark glasses happened into Greg's tunnel. The rabbit's name was Jack. Jack said, "What a hoot! You're the old coot—the groundhog that went missing. It's oh so cold, man. We need you to come out."

Greg just grumped and grumbled. Jack laughed and said, "Do not frown. I'll set your clock for late winter. And when it rings, together we will go up and jump start spring.

If Greg doesn't come out, it will always be winter. Spring will never come.[1] What did Jack do to get Greg ready to go above ground?[2]

14

❶ **Teacher Think Aloud**

❷ **Inferring, Explaining** (Jack set Greg's alarm clock.)

STORY COMPREHENSION

Use work pages from the workbook.

UNIT 36 COMPREHENSION WORK ACTIVITY 4 Name ____________________
For use after Story 4

The Grumpy Groundhog
A Foolish Fear

Identifying—Who

1. Who is the story about?
   - ● a grumpy groundhog and a rabbit
   - ○ a flying fish and a grumpy dog
   - ○ a grumpy cow and a rabbit

Writing
Identifying—Problem
Conventions—Period

2. What is the problem? Greg, the groundhog, stayed underground, so spring had never come.

Tracing
Writing
Describing
Conventions—Period

3. Who is Jack? (Accept any reasonable response.)
   Jack is a hip gray rabbit.

Tracing
Writing
Identifying—What
Conventions—Period

4. What did Jack say? Look in your book. (Accept any reasonable response.)
   Jack said, "What a hoot! You're the old coot."

65

CHECKOUT OPPORTUNITY

Listen to your students read individually while others work.

PROCEDURES

For each step, demonstrate and guide practice as needed.

1. Multiple Choice—Basic Instructions (Item 1)

Have students fill in the bubble for the correct answer.

2. Sentence Completion—Basic Instructions (Items 2, 3, 4)

- In Items 2–3, have students read and complete the sentence, ending with a period.
- In Item 4, point out the quotation marks and explain that they mean someone is talking. Explain that the words inside the quotations are what someone says.
  Have students trace the sentence beginning and write the end of the sentence. (Students may choose to write more than one sentence.)

1 SOUND REVIEW

2 SOUNDING OUT SMOOTHLY

Provide repeated practice. Mix group and individual turns, independent of your voice.

◆◆ 3 ACCURACY AND FLUENCY BUILDING

- Repeat practice on each column, building accuracy first and then fluency.
- Have students identify which words rhyme.

◆◆ 4 MULTISYLLABIC WORDS

★ **New word ending: /-ly/**

- Have students look at the first word in the Hearts Row. Say something like:

  See if you can figure out your new word, but keep it a secret.
  Now, tell me the word. (really)
  Yes, the word is "really." I *really* like your hard work.
  So what does l-y say? (/-ly/)
  You just figured out that l-y says /-ly/.

- Have students say each word part, then read the whole word. Use the words in sentences as needed.
- Provide repeated practice. Mix group and individual turns, independent of your voice.

5 CONTRACTIONS

★ **New contractions: "I'll," "don't"**

- To introduce the contractions, say something like:

  Read the first two words. (I will)
  A short way to say "I will" is the next word. Sound it out in your head.
  Remember, you just sound out as if the little mark—the apostrophe—wasn't there.
  What's the word? (I'll) You can say, "I *will* read the story" or . . . "*I'll* read the story."

- Repeat with "do not" and "don't."

6 MORE ACCURACY AND FLUENCY BUILDING

- For the word "strike," remind students that when the letter e is at the end of a word, it often gets bossy. Tell them that the Bossy E jumps right over the k and makes the underlined letter say its name.
- Have students say the underlined part, then read the word.
- Provide repeated practice. Mix group and individual turns, independent of your voice.

◆◆ 7 TRICKY WORDS

Have students read the rows. Repeat, mixing group and individual turns, independent of your voice. Use the words in sentences as needed.

8 DAILY STORY READING

Proceed to the Unit 36 Storybook. See Daily Lesson Planning for pacing suggestions.

9 COMPREHENSION AND SKILL WORK ACTIVITY 5 AND/OR ACTIVITY 6

See pages 43–44, 45, and/or 49.

◆◆ For ELLs and children with language delays, provide repeated and extended practice with the language patterns. See page 10 for tips.

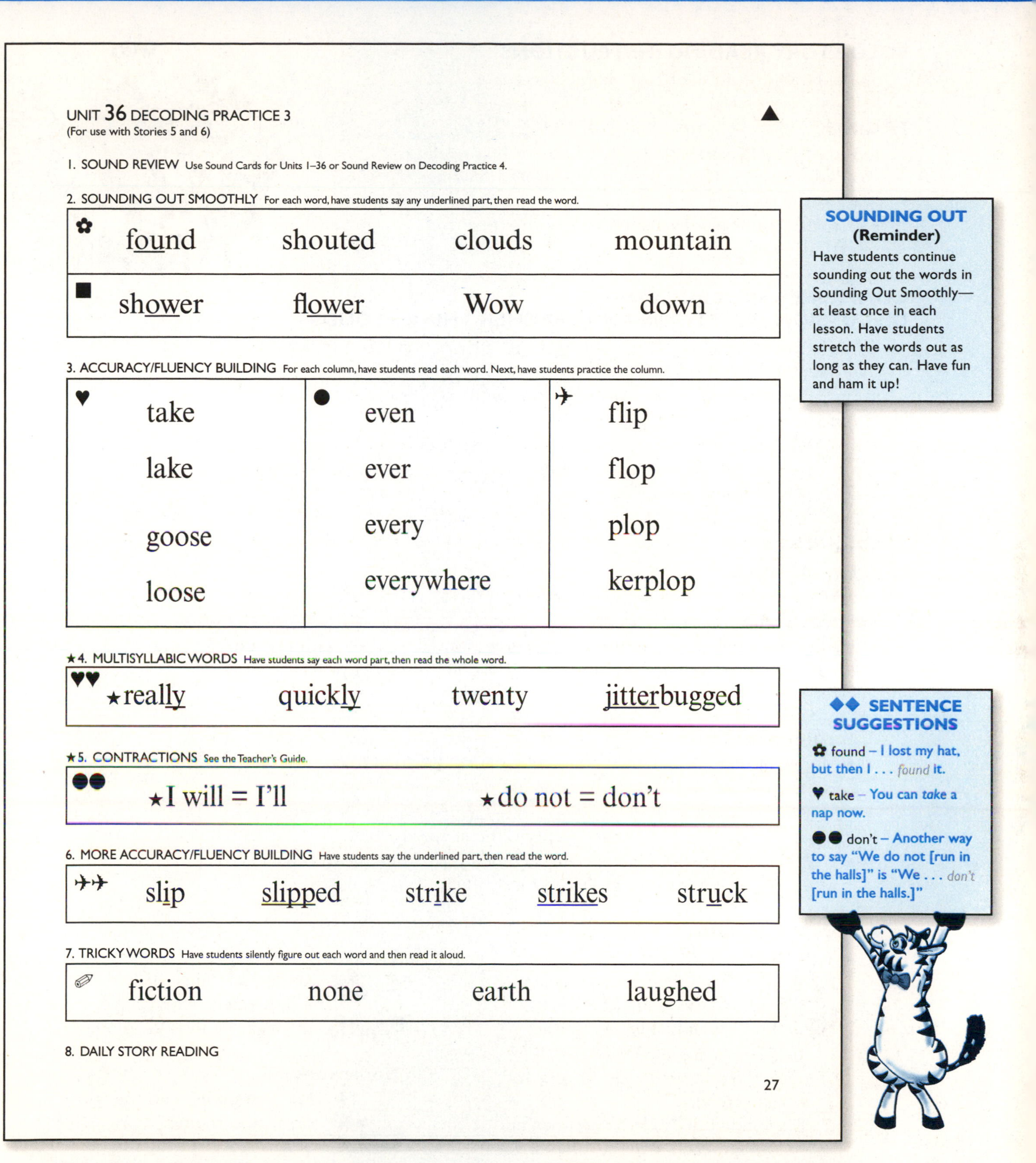

UNIT 36 DECODING PRACTICE 3 ▲
(For use with Stories 5 and 6)

1. SOUND REVIEW Use Sound Cards for Units 1–36 or Sound Review on Decoding Practice 4.

2. SOUNDING OUT SMOOTHLY For each word, have students say any underlined part, then read the word.

✿	found	shouted	clouds	mountain
■	shower	flower	Wow	down

3. ACCURACY/FLUENCY BUILDING For each column, have students read each word. Next, have students practice the column.

♥	●	✈
take	even	flip
lake	ever	flop
goose	every	plop
loose	everywhere	kerplop

★4. MULTISYLLABIC WORDS Have students say each word part, then read the whole word.

♥♥	★really	quickly	twenty	jitterbugged

★5. CONTRACTIONS See the Teacher's Guide.

●●	★I will = I'll	★do not = don't

6. MORE ACCURACY/FLUENCY BUILDING Have students say the underlined part, then read the word.

✈✈	slip	slipped	strike	strikes	struck

7. TRICKY WORDS Have students silently figure out each word and then read it aloud.

✏	fiction	none	earth	laughed

8. DAILY STORY READING

27

SOUNDING OUT
(Reminder)
Have students continue sounding out the words in Sounding Out Smoothly—at least once in each lesson. Have students stretch the words out as long as they can. Have fun and ham it up!

◆◆ SENTENCE SUGGESTIONS

✿ found – I lost my hat, but then I . . . *found* it.

♥ take – You can *take* a nap now.

●● don't – Another way to say "We do not [run in the halls]" is "We . . . *don't* [run in the halls.]"

Sentence Suggestions: Use the appropriate suggested sentence *after* decoding each individual word.

SOLO STORY READING INSTRUCTIONS

Students read from their own storybooks.

PACING

- 3- to 4-Day Plans: Have students do the first reading of Solo Story 5. Then proceed to repeated readings of Solo Story 6.
- 6- to 10-Day Plans: Have students do the first *and* second readings.

COMPREHENSION BUILDING: DISCUSSION QUESTIONS AND TEACHER THINK ALOUDS

- Ask questions and discuss text on the *second* reading when indicated in the storybook in light gray text.
- Encourage students to answer questions with complete sentences and to elaborate when appropriate.
- If students have difficulty with a comprehension question, think aloud with them or reread the portion of the story that answers the question. Then, ask the question again.

PROCEDURES

1. First Reading

- Have students individually whisper read the story, using their fingers to track text.
- After students complete the first reading and before the second reading, have students practice a paragraph. First demonstrate expressive reading for students, then give individual turns. Acknowledge student efforts.

2. Second Reading

- Mix group and individual turns, independent of your voice. Have students work toward an accuracy goal of 0–2 errors. Quietly keep track of errors made by all students in each group.
- After reading the story, practice any difficult words.
- If the group has not reached the accuracy goal, have the group reread the story, mixing group and individual turns.

3. Repeated Readings

a. Timed Readings

- Once the accuracy goal has been achieved, have individual students read the page while the other children track the text with their fingers and whisper read.
  Time individuals for 30 seconds and encourage each student to work for a personal best.
- Determine words correct per minute. Record student scores.

b. Partner Reading

During students' daily independent work, have them do Partner Reading.

c. Homework 3

Have students read the story at home. (A reprint of this story is available on a blackline master in *Read Well Homework*.)

STORY 5, SOLO

CHAPTER 2

A Sunny Winter Day

Do you think Greg will leave his tunnel when the clock rings?[1] Do you think he will run back underground if he sees his shadow?[2]

Jack Rabbit and the grumpy old groundhog, Greg, were tucked underground. Jack said, "When the clock rings, we are going out on the town. There will be no more of this foolish hanging around in the dark."

Greg just grumped and grumbled.

Did Greg want to go outdoors? Why not?[3]

❶ **Predicting**

❷ **Predicting**

❸ **Inferring, Explaining** (No, Greg didn't want to go out. He was afraid he would see his shadow.)

STORY 5, SOLO

All of a sudden, the clock rang. Jack jumped and shouted, "That's it, man. We are going to jump start spring." Jack plopped his dark glasses on Greg and did a little jitterbug. Before Greg could mutter a sound, Jack scooted him around. Then as quick as a wink, they were up on the ground.

When the clock rang, what did Jack do?[1]

Groundhog Greg looked at the sun. There were no clouds in the sky. There was no big black thing. The dark glasses kept him from seeing his foolish fear. Greg giggled, then shouted, "Come on spring!"

Jack jitterbugged some more and said, "You did it, man."

Greg had a foolish fear of his shadow. How did Jack keep Greg from being afraid of his shadow?[2]

Now, thanks to Jack, groundhogs are happy to set their clocks and wish for spring. With no more foolish fear, they pop up out of their tunnels when their clocks ring.

Did this story have a happy ending?[3] According to this story, why does spring come every year?[4] Do you think this story is fact or fiction?[5]

We learned earlier that some people say if a groundhog comes out of his hole in the winter and sees his shadow, he will go back in his hole and winter will continue. Do you think this saying is fact or fiction?[6]

16

1. **Identifying—Action** (Jack put his dark glasses on Greg. Then he grabbed Greg and took him above ground.)
2. **Inferring** (Jack put dark glasses on Greg, so he couldn't see his shadow.)
3. **Inferring, Explaining** (Greg went above ground. He didn't see his shadow, so he was happy.)
4. **Inferring, Explaining** (Spring comes every year because Greg comes out of his hole and doesn't see his shadow.)
5. **Inferring, Classifying**
6. **Teacher Think Aloud, Inferring, Classifying**

STORY 5, SOLO
COME ON SPRING!
17

COMPREHENSION BUILDING: ORAL STORY RETELL

- Have students study the pictures, then ask questions and discuss the pictures as indicated in the storybook in light gray text. The circle, square, and triangle provide visual references for the beginning, middle, and end of the story.

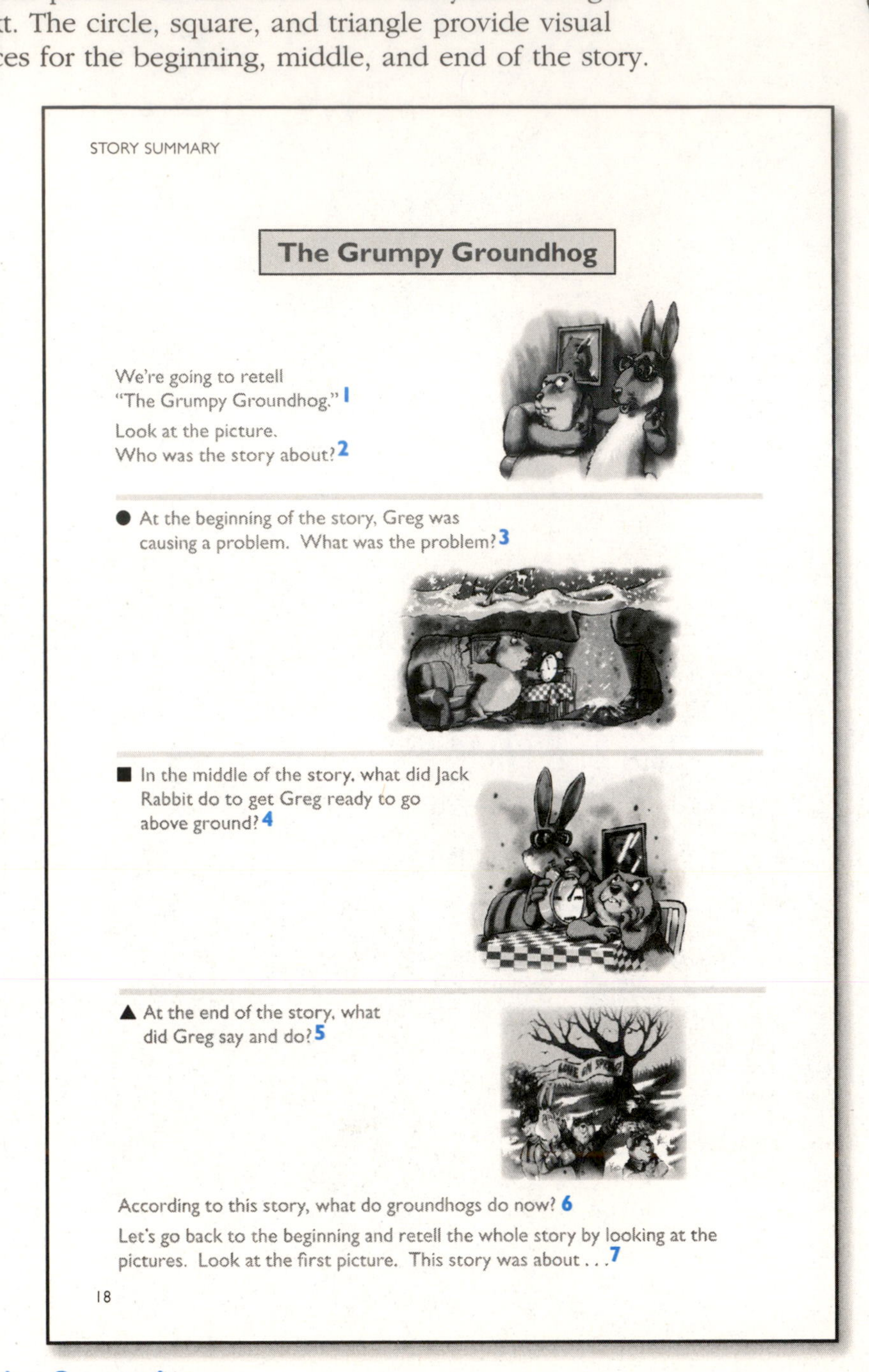

STORY SUMMARY

The Grumpy Groundhog

We're going to retell "The Grumpy Groundhog." 1
Look at the picture.
Who was the story about? 2

● At the beginning of the story, Greg was causing a problem. What was the problem? 3

■ In the middle of the story, what did Jack Rabbit do to get Greg ready to go above ground? 4

▲ At the end of the story, what did Greg say and do? 5

According to this story, what do groundhogs do now? 6
Let's go back to the beginning and retell the whole story by looking at the pictures. Look at the first picture. This story was about . . . 7

18

❶ **Summarizing, Sequencing**

❷ **Identifying—Who** (The story was about a grumpy groundhog named Greg and a rabbit named Jack.)

❸ **Explaining—Beginning, Problem** (Greg was afraid of his shadow and didn't want to go above ground, so spring had never come.)

❹ **Explaining—Middle, Action** (Jack set Greg's alarm for late winter and told him he would take Greg out on the town.)

❺ **Explaining—End** (At the end, Greg went above ground. He giggled and said, "Come on spring!")

❻ **Explaining** (Now groundhogs pop up out of their tunnels when their clocks ring.)

❼ **Summarizing**

STORY MAP

Use work pages from the workbook.

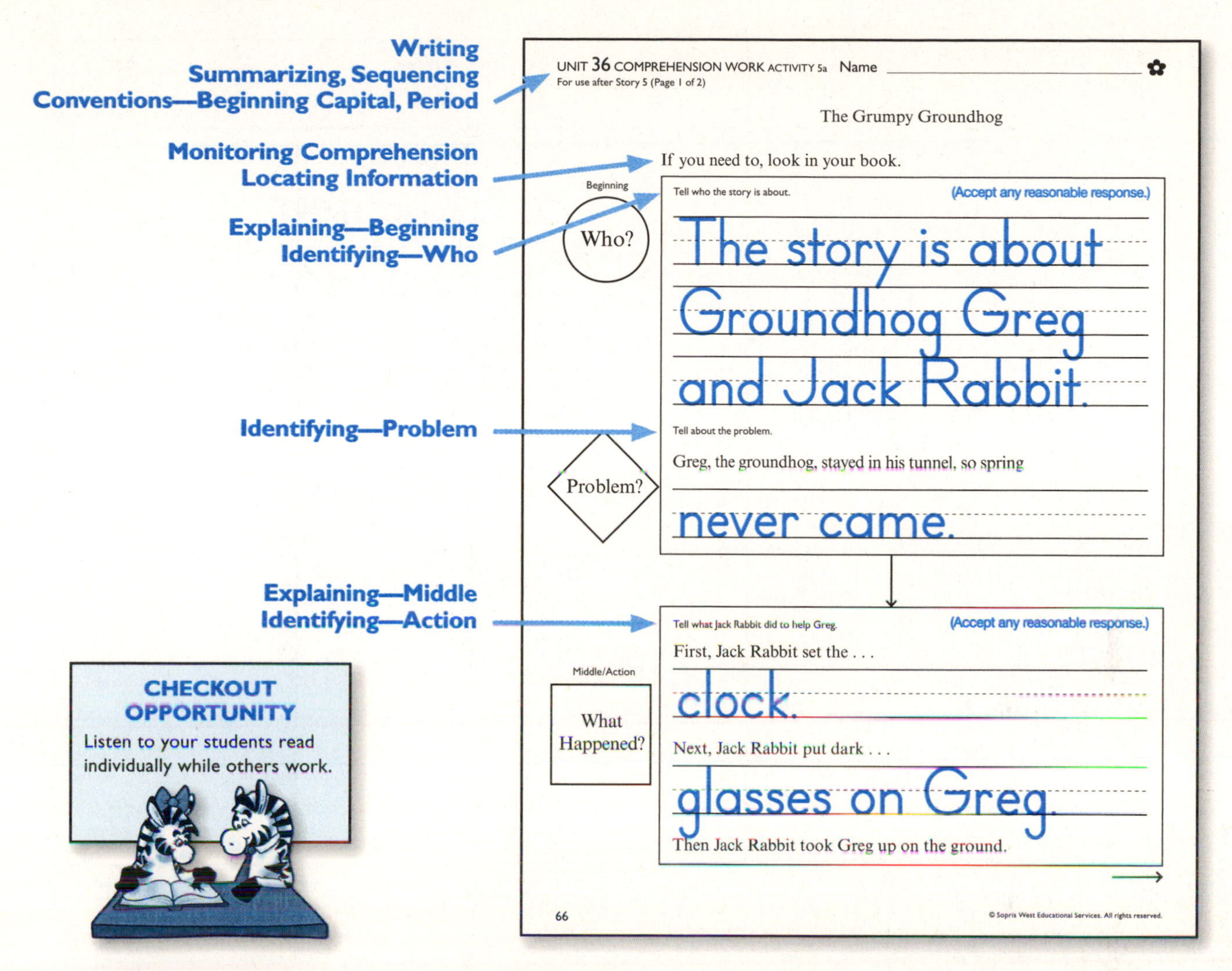

UNIT 36 COMPREHENSION WORK ACTIVITY 5a Name ______

For use after Story 5 (Page 1 of 2)

The Grumpy Groundhog

If you need to, look in your book.

Beginning — Who?

Tell who the story is about. (Accept any reasonable response.)

The story is about Groundhog Greg and Jack Rabbit.

Problem?

Tell about the problem.

Greg, the groundhog, stayed in his tunnel, so spring never came.

Middle/Action — What Happened?

Tell what Jack Rabbit did to help Greg. (Accept any reasonable response.)

First, Jack Rabbit set the . . . clock.

Next, Jack Rabbit put dark . . . glasses on Greg.

Then Jack Rabbit took Greg up on the ground.

66

© Sopris West Educational Services. All rights reserved.

PROCEDURES

For each step, demonstrate and guide practice as needed.

Story Map—Basic Instructions

- Using a blank or overhead copy of the story map, help students identify the basic story elements—who the story is about, what the problem was, what happened in the story, and what happened at the end.
- Have students fill in the blanks to create a story map of "The Grumpy Groundhog."
- Remind students that a story map helps them retell or summarize the important parts of a story.

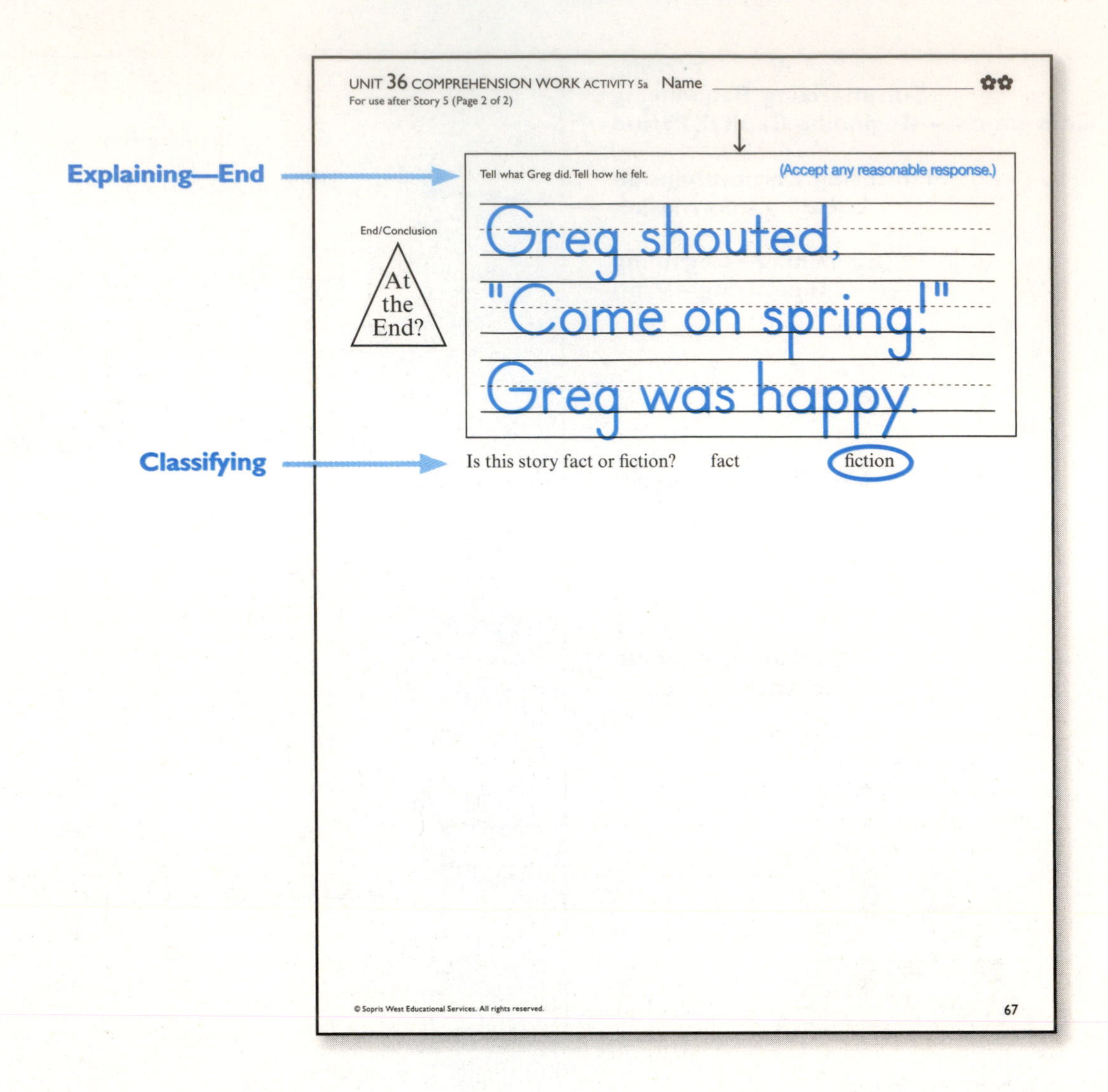
Explaining—End
Classifying
UNIT 36 COMPREHENSION WORK ACTIVITY 5a Name
For use after Story 5 (Page 2 of 2)
Tell what Greg did. Tell how he felt.
(Accept any reasonable response.)
End/Conclusion
At the End?
Greg shouted,
"Come on spring!"
Greg was happy.
Is this story fact or fiction? fact fiction
© Sopris West Educational Services. All rights reserved.
67

RHYMING PATTERNS

Use work pages from the workbook.

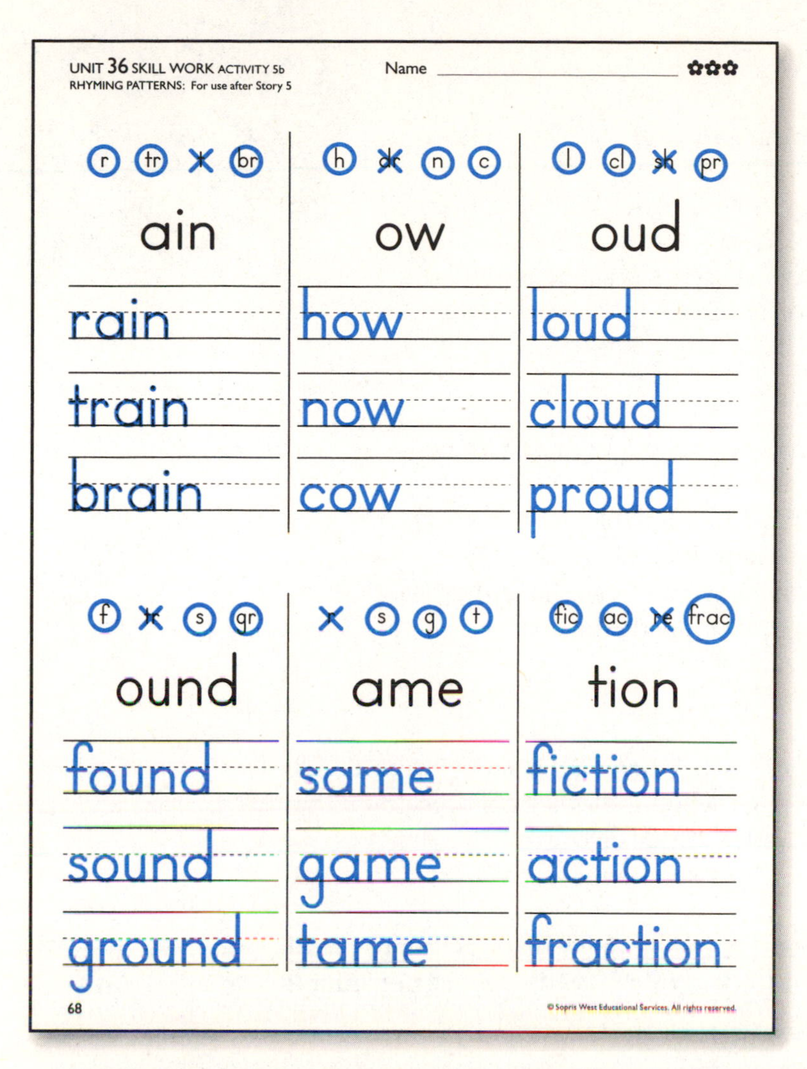

UNIT 36 SKILL WORK ACTIVITY 5b Name ______________________
RHYMING PATTERNS: For use after Story 5

r tr x br — **ain**: rain, train, brain

h x n c — **ow**: how, now, cow

l cl x pr — **oud**: loud, cloud, proud

f x s gr — **ound**: found, sound, ground

x s g t — **ame**: same, game, tame

fic ac x frac — **tion**: fiction, action, fraction

68

PROCEDURES

Demonstrate and guide practice as needed.

Rhyming Patterns—Basic Instructions

For each box, have students:

- Read the rhyming pattern.
- Circle the three sounds above the rhyming pattern that go with it to make real words.
- Cross out the sound that does not make a real word with the rhyming pattern.
- Write the three rhyming words on the lines provided.

Note: For students who struggle or who lack the English language base to know which are real words, you may wish to identify the three sounds they should circle in each box. Students can then write the pattern words on their own.

SOLO STORY READING INSTRUCTIONS

Students read from their own storybooks.

PROCEDURES

1. First Reading

- Have students individually whisper read the story, using their fingers to track text.
- After students complete the first reading and before the second reading, have students identify the words that rhyme in each verse. Then have students practice a few verses. Demonstrate expressive reading for students, then give individual turns. Acknowledge student efforts.

2. Second Reading

- Mix group and individual turns, independent of your voice. Have students work toward an accuracy goal of 0–2 errors. Quietly keep track of errors made by all students in each group.
- After reading the story, practice any difficult words.
- If the group has not reached the accuracy goal, have the group reread the story, mixing group and individual turns.

3. Repeated Readings

a. Timed Readings

- Once the accuracy goal has been achieved, have individual students read the page while the other children track the text with their fingers and whisper read.

Time individuals for 30 seconds and encourage each student to work for a personal best.

- Count the number of words read correctly in 30 seconds (words read minus errors). Multiply by two to determine words correct per minute. Record student scores.

b. Partner Reading

During students' daily independent work, have them do Partner Reading.

c. Homework 4

Have students read the story at home. (A reprint of this story is available on a blackline master in *Read Well* Homework.)

STORY 6, SOLO

Flip, Flop, Kerplop

Plop, drop, kerplop,
Wow! Wow! My, my!
An afternoon shower
Falls from the sky.

Plop, drop, flip, flop,
What's raining down?
Raindrops, raindrops,
All around the town.

Flip, flop, kerplop,
Is it raining fish?
See the rain wiggle,
Hear it swish!

Plop, drop, kerplop,
You silly goose!
It isn't raining fish.
Fish are not on the loose.

STORY 6, SOLO

Plop, drop, flip, flop,
They don't stop!
Green, green raindrops,
That hop, hop, hop!

Plop, drop, kerplop,
Frogs are everywhere!
It's raining frogs.
Look! See them there.

Plop, drop, flip, flop,
Now I've seen it all,
Frogs in the clouds
And frogs that fall.

Flip, flop, kerplop,
Now it's sunny.
Frogs on the ground,
How very, very funny.

20

FOCUS ON EXPRESSION

After the first reading, have students practice one or two verses at a time. Demonstrate how to read the poem within the children's reading rate, but with the rhythm and cadence of a poem. Avoid an overly sing-songy voice.

STORY COMPREHENSION

Use work pages from the workbook.

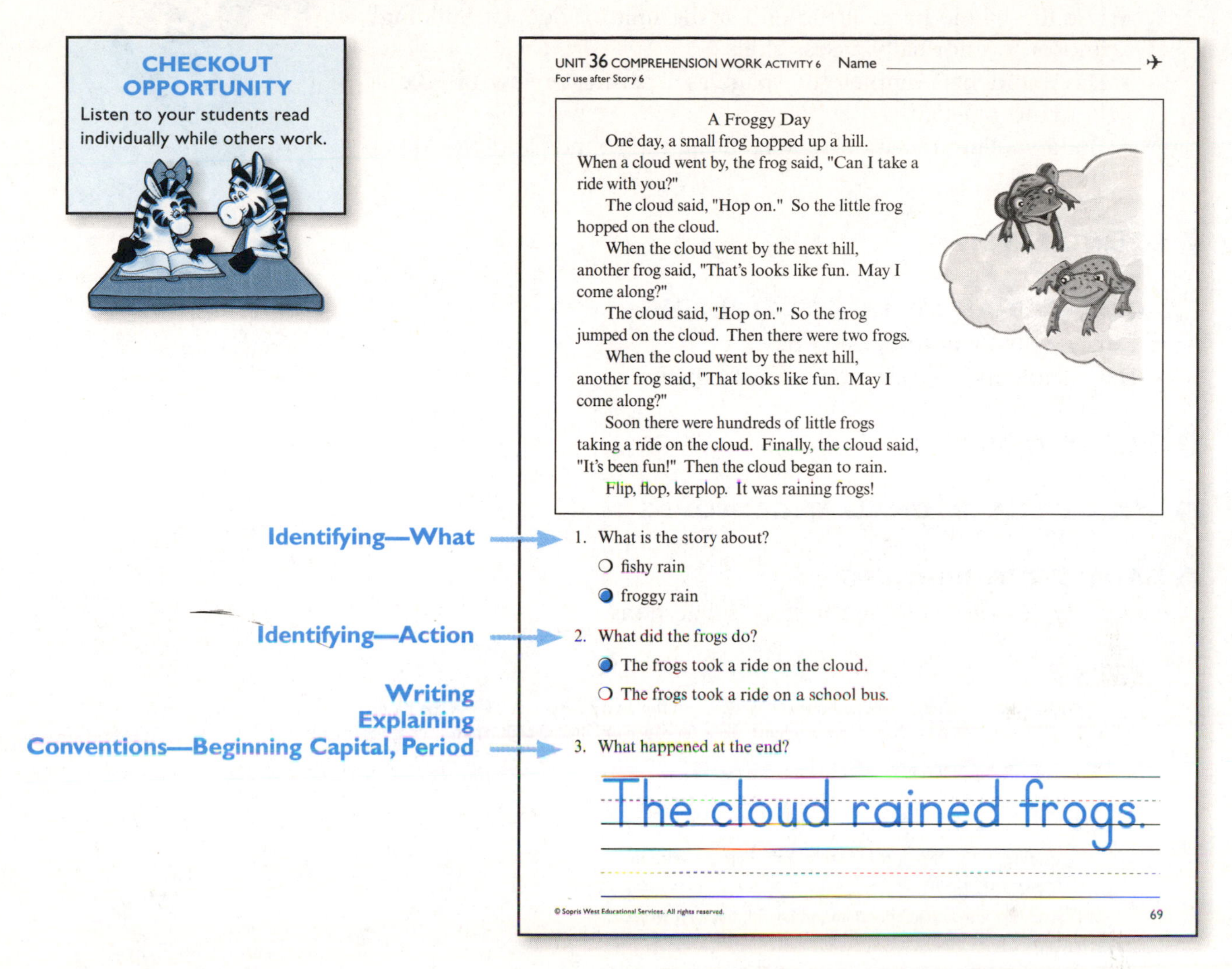

UNIT 36 COMPREHENSION WORK ACTIVITY 6 Name ____________

For use after Story 6

A Froggy Day

One day, a small frog hopped up a hill. When a cloud went by, the frog said, "Can I take a ride with you?"

The cloud said, "Hop on." So the little frog hopped on the cloud.

When the cloud went by the next hill, another frog said, "That's looks like fun. May I come along?"

The cloud said, "Hop on." So the frog jumped on the cloud. Then there were two frogs.

When the cloud went by the next hill, another frog said, "That looks like fun. May I come along?"

Soon there were hundreds of little frogs taking a ride on the cloud. Finally, the cloud said, "It's been fun!" Then the cloud began to rain.

Flip, flop, kerplop. It was raining frogs!

1. What is the story about?
   - ○ fishy rain
   - ● froggy rain
2. What did the frogs do?
   - ● The frogs took a ride on the cloud.
   - ○ The frogs took a ride on a school bus.
3. What happened at the end?

   The cloud rained frogs.

© Sopris West Educational Services. All rights reserved. 69

PROCEDURES

For each step, demonstrate and guide practice as needed.

Paragraph Comprehension—Basic Instructions

- Have students read the paragraph to themselves.
- Have students fill in the bubbles for the correct answers.
- Have students write a complete sentence that starts with a capital letter and ends with a period.

Note: There are multiple uses for Decoding Practice 4.

- Have students practice a few rows and/or columns each day.
- Use the whole page at the end of the unit for fluency building and/or to informally assess skills.
- Have students complete the page as a partner review or take it home to practice.
- Build spelling dictation lessons using the sounds and words on this page.

❶ SOUND REVIEW

❷ ACCURACY AND FLUENCY BUILDING

- Build accuracy and then fluency.
- Have students identify which words rhyme.

❸ TRICKY WORDS

❹ MULTISYLLABIC CHALLENGE WORDS

❺ DAILY STORY READING

See Daily Lesson Planning for story suggestions.

BOSSY E

If students would benefit from additional practice with the Bossy E Rule, reinforce the patterns /a_e/ and /i_e/ with dictation. Have students work on paper or small chalkboards.

Demonstrate and guide practice as needed.

- Say the word. Use it in a sentence. Have students tell you the word.
  The word is "came." We *came* to school.
- Ask students what the first sound is. Tell them to write it.
  Tell me the first sound. /c/ Write it.
- Ask students what the second sound is. Tell them to write it.
  Tell me the next sound. /ăăă/ Write it.
- Ask students what the third sound is. Tell them to write it.
  Tell me the last sound. /mmm/ Write it.
- Tell students what they've written. (Pronounce the consonant-vowel-consonant, or CVC, word.)
  You've written /căm/.
- Ask students what they need to make the word say "came."
  What does the word need to make it say "came"? (The Bossy E)
- Repeat the word with several other /a_e/ and /i_e /words.

UNIT 36 DECODING PRACTICE 4 ✈
(See Daily Lesson Planning for story suggestions.)

1. SOUND REVIEW Set pace. Have students read the sounds in each row.

▲	ou	Z	r	u	j	sh	L	7
■	v	i	b	T	ow	c	ay	14
●	x	th	er	y	s	Qu	H	21

2. ACCURACY/FLUENCY BUILDING For each column, have students say any underlined part, then read each word. Next, have students read the column.

✈	✈✈	✿	✿✿	✿✿✿
sound	funny	clown	dame	Who
pound	sunny	frown	rat	What
mound	cloudy	flower	base	Where
ground	rainy	shower	cape	Why
around	easy	power	man	When

3. TRICKY WORDS Have students silently figure out each word and then read it aloud.

☆☆	water	laugh	gone	their	about
☆☆☆	very	has	were	one	many

4. MULTISYLLABIC CHALLENGE WORDS Have students say each word part, then read the whole word.

ten•der•ly = tenderly	outdoors
fool•ish•ly = foolishly	outfit
happ•i•ly = happily	outstanding

5. DAILY STORY READING

28

CULMINATING ACTIVITIES (Reminder)

As culminating activities:

- Have students identify rhyming words.
- Have students find small words in big words.
- Have students pick a column or row to read.

End of the Unit

In this section, you will find:

Making Decisions

As you near the end of the unit, you will need to make decisions. Should you administer the Oral Reading Fluency Assessment or should you teach Extra Practice lessons?

Unit 36 Oral Reading Fluency Assessment

The Unit 36 Oral Reading Fluency Assessment is located on page 54 and can also be found in the *Assessment Manual.*

Certificate of Achievement

Celebrate your children's accomplishments.

Decoding Diagnosis

If students have difficulty passing the assessment, the Decoding Diagnosis can be used to more accurately diagnose specific problems.

Extra Practice

Lessons and blackline masters for added decoding practice and independent work are provided for students who need extended practice opportunities.

Making Decisions

ASSESSMENT READINESS

Assess when students are able to easily complete decoding tasks from the beginning of a lesson.

- If you aren't sure whether students are ready for the assessment, give the assessment. Do Extra Practice lessons if needed.
- If students are not ready for the assessment, proceed to Extra Practice lessons. Administer the assessment as soon as students are ready.

GENERAL ASSESSMENT GUIDELINES

- Assess all students.
- Assess each child individually.
- Score student responses on the Student Assessment Record, adhering to the scoring criteria in the *Assessment Manual*. Use a stopwatch to time how long it takes the student to read the oral fluency passage.
- Follow the general instructions at the bottom of each assessment. Record a Strong Pass, a Pass, a Weak Pass, or a No Pass.

ACCELERATION

- If students read with 100% accuracy and exceed the fluency goal, consider shortening units.
- If an individual student reads with greater fluency than others in his or her group, consider regrouping.

ASSESSING UNPRACTICED READING

Do not have children practice the assessments. The goal of reading instruction is to provide children with the skills to read independently. Repeated readings are an excellent tool for building fluency; however, the end-of-the-unit assessment is designed to assess how well students transfer their skills to unrehearsed passages.

INTERVENTION OPTIONS—INDIVIDUALS (WEAK PASS, NO PASS)

1. Add informal practice throughout the day.
2. Add practice with repeated readings on Solo Stories.
3. Find ways to provide a double dose of *Read Well* instruction.
   - Have the student work in his or her group *and* a lower group.
   - Have an instructional assistant, older student, or parent volunteer preview or review lessons.
   - Have an instructional assistant provide instruction with Extra Practice lessons.
4. Consider placement in a lower group. If one child's fluency scores are significantly lower than the other children in the group, success will be impossible without additional and intensive practice.

INTERVENTION OPTIONS—GROUP (WEAK PASS, NO PASS)

1. Extend the unit with Extra Practice lessons.
2. Consider a Jell-Well Review before moving forward. (See the *Assessment Manual*.)

CERTIFICATE OF ACHIEVEMENT

When students pass the assessment, celebrate with the Certificate of Achievement. Then, set a personal goal. (See *Getting Started*.)

CRITICAL ASSESSMENT

TRICKY WORD WARM-UP

their	any	everywhere	what	laughed

ORAL READING FLUENCY PASSAGE

My Missing Cat

★I keep my cat indoors. However, last week he got out. 11
He ran away for two days. We went all around town shouting 23
his name. He couldn't be found. 29

So we ran an ad for the cat. The next day, a man came 43
to the door with my cat. That funny cat didn't even make a 56
sound. He just jumped down from the man's arms and quickly 67
ran to me. I was very happy to have my cat back. He had a 82
big snack, and then he went to sleep on my lap. 93

ORAL READING FLUENCY Start timing at the ★. Mark errors. Make a single slash in the text (/) at 60 seconds. Have student complete passage. If the student completes the passage in less than 60 seconds, have the student go back to the ★ and continue reading. Make a double slash (//) in the text at 60 seconds.

WCPM Determine words correct per minute by subtracting errors from words read in 60 seconds.

STRONG PASS The student scores no more than 2 errors on the first pass through the passage and reads a minimum of 95 or more words correct per minute. Proceed to Unit 37.

PASS The student scores no more than 2 errors on the first pass through the passage and reads 76 to 94 words correct per minute. Proceed to Unit 37.

WEAK PASS The student scores no more than 2 errors on the first pass through the passage and reads 58 to 75 words correct per minute. Proceed to Unit 37 with added fluency practice, or provide Extra Practice lessons in Unit 36, and/or provide a Jell-Well Review.

NO PASS The student scores 3 or more errors on the first pass through the passage and/or reads 57 or fewer words correct per minute. Provide Extra Practice lessons and retest, and/or provide a Jell-Well Review.

Certificate of Achievement

This certifies that

____,

on this ________________ day of ________________, _____,

has successfully completed

Read Well Unit 36

Sounds Mastered: s, e, ee, m, a, d, th, n, t, w, i, Th, h, c, r, ea, sh, k, -ck, oo, ar, wh, ĕ, -y (as in "fly"), l, o, b, all, g, f, u, -er, oo (as in "book"), y, a (schwa), p, ay, v, qu, j, x, or, z, a_e, -y (as in "baby"), i_e, ou, ow

Known Words: By Unit 35, you had learned and practiced 1,251 words.

New Words Mastered in Unit 36: again, don't, English, everywhere, goose, I'll, laugh, laughed, loose, rain, raindrops, rained, raining, rainy, woman, around, base, brown, cars, clocks, cloud, clouds, cloudy, clown, coot, cow, dame, dig, dogs, down, easy, expected, fallen, falls, fifty, flip, flop, flower, foolishly, found, froggy, frown, glasses, grabbed, Greg, Greg's, ground, groundhog, groundhogs, hands, happened, happening, happily, houses, how, however, indoor, jitterbugged, kerplop, loud, lumps, mound, mountain, now, oddest, out, outdoors, outfit, outstanding, planet, plenty, plop, popped, pound, power, quickly, rabbit's, really, round, safety, seventy, shelter, shout, shouted, shower, silly, sixty, slip, slipped, sound, sounds, streets, stike, strikes, struck, sucked, summer, take, tenderly, thousands, torn, town, twenty, underground, upon, wiggle, winds, winter, wow

You can now read 1,360 words—plus many other words made up of the sounds and patterns you've learned.

Note: Personal and Team Goal Setting forms can be copied from Units 16 and 17, or from *Getting Started.*

Decoding Diagnosis

If students have difficulty passing the Oral Reading Fluency Assessment, the Decoding Diagnosis can be used to more accurately diagnose specific problems. A Decoding Diagnosis is included in the *Assessment Manual* and the Teacher's Guides for Units 19, 23, 26, 28, 30, 34, 36, and 38.

Note: If a student is unable to meet the oral reading fluency goal, he or she may have been misplaced initially, or instruction may have proceeded too fast in the earlier units. If the student makes errors related to one or two skills, you may be able to remediate these skills with intensive work. However, if the student is weak on three or more skills, he or she will need either a careful Jell-Well Review or placement in a lower group.

PROCEDURES FOR ADMINISTERING A DECODING DIAGNOSIS

1. Have the student read from the Decoding Diagnosis. Score on a separate copy.
2. For each subtest, have the student point to and read each item.
3. Make a slash through any item missed and record what the student said above the missed item.

GUIDELINES FOR REMEDIATING SPECIFIC SKILLS

Sounds

- If the student misses only one sound, continue to the next unit but provide additional practice on the difficult sound.
- If the student makes more than one error, consider placing the student in a lower group, providing a Jell-Well Review, or systematically reintroducing one new difficult sound at a time.

Vowel Discriminations

- Have the student practice words that require vowel discrimination. Build lists of words composed of known sounds, with only the vowel changing (e.g., m<u>e</u>t, m<u>a</u>t, m<u>ea</u>t). See the subtest examples.
- Provide additional practice on all the vowel sounds taught to date. Reteach all vowel units, while continuously reviewing all known sounds.

Beginning Quick Sounds

- Have the student practice pairs of rhyming words in which one word begins with a quick sound (e.g., went-<u>d</u>ent, sand-<u>h</u>and).
- Have the student practice lists of words that begin with one quick sound (e.g., had-hid-hard).
- Reteach all units that introduce a quick sound, and review all known sounds.

Blends and Word Endings

- Have the student read lists of words that increase in length, and which include difficult blends and/or word endings (e.g., ack-nack-snack, kitt-kitten).
- Dictate words that build up (e.g., in, ink, sink, rink, drink).

Tricky Words

- Identify the difficult words and increase practice on one difficult word at a time.
- Have the student write any difficult word and use it in a sentence.

SOUNDS

S	ea	ou	o	x	n	t	qu
i	z	c	r	ow	oo	K	ar

VOWEL DISCRIMINATION

bay	bar	bee	boo	by
eat	at	it	art	out

BEGINNING QUICK SOUNDS

town	jar	dog	pound	base
gun	bead	win	kiss	howl

BLENDS AND WORD ENDINGS

fact	raining	drops	sky	waves
ground	happy	little	darken	example

TRICKY WORDS

laughed	rain	father	any	your
their	very	learned	come	they

- Have students read from a clean copy of the Decoding Diagnosis. Record incorrect responses on another copy.
- Use information from both the Unit 36 Decoding Assessment and the Unit 36 Decoding Diagnosis to identify specific skill deficits.

❶ SOUNDS

❷ WORD DICTATION

how, out, keep, just

The first word is "how." We're going to count the sounds in "how."
Tell me the first sound. **Hold up one finger.** (/h/)
Tell me the next sound. **Hold up two fingers.** (/ow/)
How many sounds are in "how"? (Two)

Tell me the first sound. (/h/) Write it.
Tell me the next sound. (/ow/) Write it with the letter o and the letter w.
Do Smooth Blending. (/how/) Read the word. (how)

Repeat with "out," "keep," and "just." Tell students that /ou/ in "out" is spelled with the letters o and u.

CAUTION

Your children may not need Extra Practice. If in doubt, assess students and include Extra Practice only if needed.

DICTATION

- Demonstrate and guide practice as needed.
- Have students check and correct.

❸ SENTENCE COMPLETION

My cat sat *on my lap.*

- Have students read the beginning of the sentence with you.
- Dictate the last three words, "on my lap." Remind students to leave a finger space between each word.
- Have students trace the dotted words and complete the sentence with a period.
- Have students read the sentence.

❹ ACCURACY AND FLUENCY BUILDING

Repeat practice on each column, building accuracy first and then fluency.

❺ TRICKY WORDS

Repeat practice, mixing group and individual turns, independent of your voice.

❻ DAILY STORY READING

1. First Reading

Have students choral read the Fluency Passage.

2. Second Reading

- Provide individual turns on sentences. Quietly keep track of errors.
- After reading, practice any difficult words.

3. Repeated Readings

a. Timed Readings

- Have individual students read the passage while other students track the text with their fingers and whisper read. Time individuals for 30 seconds. Encourage students to work for a personal best.
- Determine words correct per minute. Record students' scores.

b. Partner Reading—Checkout Opportunity

While students are partner reading, listen to individuals read the passage.

UNIT 36 EXTRA PRACTICE 1 Name____________________

1. SOUNDS Have students say each sound.

ow	x	V	a	c	z	ee	-y
p	n	ay	J	o	oo	ou	or

2. WORD DICTATION Have students count the sounds in each word, identify and write each sound, and then read the words: "how," "out," "keep," and "just."

1 ____________ 2 ____________ 3 ____________ 4 ____________

3. SENTENCE COMPLETION Have students read the beginning of the sentence. Dictate "on my lap." Have students trace the words and complete the sentence with a period.

My cat sat ____________

4. ACCURACY/FLUENCY BUILDING In each column, have students say any underlined part, then read each word. Next, have students read the column.

♥	♥♥	♥♥♥
out	indoors	down
shout	however	town
sound	away	brown
found	around	clown
round	quickly	frown

5. TRICKY WORDS For each word, have students silently figure out the word, then read it aloud.

rain	their	any	laugh	couldn't

6. DAILY STORY READING

Name______________________________

FLUENCY PASSAGE

A Dark Winter Day

It was a dark winter day, so my little brother and I said, 13
"Let's stay indoors." As I made a snack for him, he started 25
yelling, "It's raining frogs!" I said he was foolish and said, 36
"When it is raining hard, you say it is raining cats and 48
dogs, not frogs!" My little brother got mad. 56

My personal best is _____ words correct per minute.
My goal is to read with 0–2 errors. This is what I did:

Reading	1st	2nd	3rd	4th
Errors				
Words/ 30 seconds				
wcpm				

Have students read the sentences. Time individual students for 30 seconds; mark errors. To determine words correct per minute (wcpm), count words read in 30 seconds, subtract errors, multiply times two, and record on the chart. If the student completes the passage in less than 30 seconds, have him or her return to the top and continue reading. (Repeated readings may be completed with older students, assistants, or parents.)

Take-Home Game

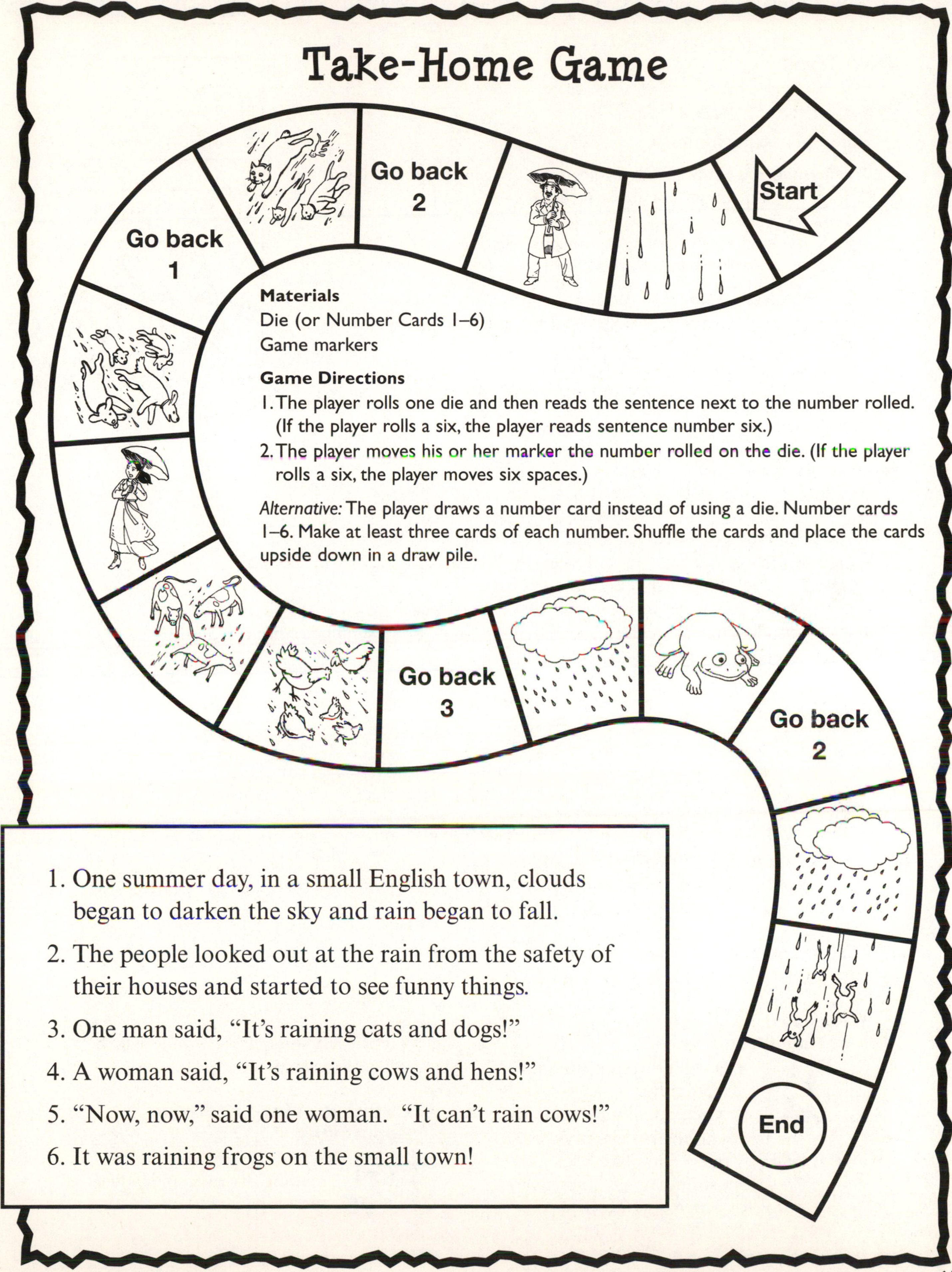

Materials

Die (or Number Cards 1–6)
Game markers

Game Directions

1. The player rolls one die and then reads the sentence next to the number rolled. (If the player rolls a six, the player reads sentence number six.)
2. The player moves his or her marker the number rolled on the die. (If the player rolls a six, the player moves six spaces.)

Alternative: The player draws a number card instead of using a die. Number cards 1–6. Make at least three cards of each number. Shuffle the cards and place the cards upside down in a draw pile.

1. One summer day, in a small English town, clouds began to darken the sky and rain began to fall.
2. The people looked out at the rain from the safety of their houses and started to see funny things.
3. One man said, "It's raining cats and dogs!"
4. A woman said, "It's raining cows and hens!"
5. "Now, now," said one woman. "It can't rain cows!"
6. It was raining frogs on the small town!

CAUTION
Your children may not need Extra Practice. If in doubt, assess students and include Extra Practice only if needed.

1 SOUNDS

2 WORD DICTATION

down, week, went, with

The first word is "down." We're going to count the sounds in "down."
Tell me the first sound. **Hold up one finger.** (/d/)
Tell me the next sound. **Hold up two fingers.** (/ow/)
Tell me the next sound. **Hold up three fingers.** (/nnn/)
How many sounds are in "down"? (Three)

Tell me the first sound. (/d/) Write it.
Tell me the next sound. (/ow/) Write it with the letter o and the letter w.
Tell me the next sound. (/nnn/) Write it.
Do Smooth Blending. (/downnn/) Read the word. (down)

Repeat with "week," "went," and "with."

3 SENTENCE COMPLETION

I didn't make *a sound.*

- Have students read the beginning of the sentence with you.
- Dictate the last two words, "a sound." Tell students that /ou/ in "sound" is spelled with the letter o and the letter u.
  Remind students to leave a finger space between each word.
- Have students trace the dotted words and complete the sentence with a period.
- Have students read the sentence.

4 ACCURACY AND FLUENCY BUILDING

5 TRICKY WORDS

6 DAILY STORY READING

1. First and Second Readings, Fluency Passage A
- Have students choral read the text.
- Provide individual turns on sentences. Quietly keep track of errors.
- After reading, practice any difficult words.

2. First and Second Readings, Fluency Passage B
Repeat step one with Fluency Passage B.

3. Repeated Readings

a. Timed Readings

- Have individual students read either passage A or B while other students track the text with their fingers and whisper read. Time individuals for 30 seconds. Encourage students to work for a personal best.
- For each student, determine words correct per minute.

b. Partner Reading—Checkout Opportunity

While students are partner reading, listen to individuals read a passage.

Name ____________________

1. SOUNDS Have students say each sound.

ou	Z	u	j	i	y	ow	-y
v	ay	ar	a	qu	er	x	e

2. WORD DICTATION Have students count the sounds in each word, identify and write each sound, and then read the words: "down," "week," "went," and "with."

1 ____________ 2 ____________ 3 ____________ 4 ____________

3. SENTENCE COMPLETION Have students read the beginning of the sentence. Dictate "a sound." Have students trace the words and complete the sentence with a period.

I didn't make ____________

4. ACCURACY/FLUENCY BUILDING In each column, have students say any underlined part, then read each word. Next, have students read the column.

♥	♥♥	♥♥♥
down	really	I'll
found	quickly	I've
frown	shouting	don't
sound	funny	couldn't
town	happy	didn't

5. TRICKY WORDS For each word, have students silently figure out the word, then read it aloud.

water	what	from	even	very

6. DAILY STORY READING

Name________________________

FLUENCY PASSAGE A

It's Raining Frogs!

After my little brother shouted that it was raining frogs, 10
he ran and took my hand. He took me to the open door 24
and said, "See!" It really was raining frogs. 31

FLUENCY PASSAGE B

Funny Weather

Last week, it rained frogs. Two days after that, it rained 11
fish! My little brother and I think it really will rain cats and 24
dogs next. We think this weather is funny! 32

My personal best is _____ words correct per minute.
My goal is to read with 0–2 errors. This is what I did:

Reading	1st	2nd	3rd	4th
Errors				
Words/ 30 seconds				
wcpm				

Have students read the sentences. Time individual students for 30 seconds on one passage; mark errors. To determine words correct per minute (wcpm), count words read in 30 seconds, subtract errors, multiply times two, and record on the chart. If the student completes the passage in less than 30 seconds, have him or her return to the top and continue reading. (Repeated readings may be completed with older students, assistants, or parents.)

❶ STORYBOOK DECODING REVIEW

For each row, mix group and individual turns, independent of your voice.

❷ WORD DICTATION

Have students count the sounds in each word with their fingers, identify and write each sound, and then read the word. Use the words in sentences as needed.

out, down, man, ran

The first word is "out." We're going to count the sounds in "out."
Tell me the first sound. **Hold up one finger.** (/ou/)
Tell me the next sound. **Hold up two fingers.** (/t/)
How many sounds are in "out"? (Two)

Tell me the first sound. (/ou/) Write it with the letter o and the letter u.
Tell me the next sound. (/t/) Write it.
Do Smooth Blending. (/out/) Read the word. (out)

Repeat with "down," "man," and "ran."
Note: Tell students that /ow/ in "down" is spelled with the letter o and the letter w.

CAUTION

Your children may not need Extra Practice. If in doubt, assess students and include Extra Practice only if needed.

❸ DAILY STORY READING

1. First Reading

Have students choral read the Fluency Passage.

2. Second Reading

- Provide individual turns on sentences. Quietly keep track of errors made by all students in the group.
- After reading, practice any difficult words.

3. Repeated Readings

a. Timed Readings

- Have individual students read the passage while other students track the text with their fingers and whisper read. Time individuals for 30 seconds. Encourage students to work for a personal best.
- For each student, count the number of words read correctly in 30 seconds (words read minus errors). Multiply by two to determine words correct per minute. Record students' scores.

b. Partner Reading—Checkout Opportunity

While students are partner reading, listen to individuals read the passage. Work on accuracy or fluency as needed.

Name______________________________

FLUENCY PASSAGE

It's Raining Frogs!

About seventy years ago, it rained frogs in a small 10
English town. Strong winds had sucked lots of little frogs 21
up into the clouds. When the rain started, the frogs fell 32
from the clouds with the rain. Soon they were hopping 41
everywhere. It was fun until they went away. We were sad 52
when they went away. 56

My personal best is _____ words correct per minute.

My goal is to read with 0–2 errors. This is what I did:

Reading	1st	2nd	3rd	4th
Errors				
Words/ 30 seconds				
wcpm				

Have students read the sentences. Time individual students for 30 seconds; mark errors. To determine words correct per minute (wcpm), count words read in 30 seconds, subtract errors, multiply times two, and record on the chart. If the student completes the passage in less than 30 seconds, have him or her return to the top and continue reading. (Repeated readings may be completed with older students, assistants, or parents.)

❶ DECODING PRACTICE 4 REVIEW

For each row, mix group and individual turns, independent of your voice.

❷ WORD DICTATION

Have students count the sounds in each word with their fingers, identify and write each sound, and then read the word. Use the words in sentences as needed.

sleep, jump, next, for

The first word is "sleep." We're going to count the sounds in "sleep."
Tell me the first sound. **Hold up one finger.** (/sss/)
Repeat with /lll/, /eeee/, and /p/.
How many sounds are in "sleep"? (Four)

Tell me the first sound. (/sss/) Write it.
Tell me the next sound. (/lll/) Write it.
Tell me the next sound. (/eeee/) Write it with two letter e's.
Tell me the next sound. (/p/) Write it.
Do Smooth Blending. (/ssslllleeeep/) Read the word. (sleep)

Repeat with "jump," "next," and "for."

CAUTION

Your children may not need Extra Practice. If in doubt, assess students and include Extra Practice only if needed.

HAVE STUDENTS CHECK AND CORRECT.

❸ DAILY STORY READING

1. First Reading

Have students choral read the Fluency Passage.

2. Second Reading

- Provide individual turns on sentences. Quietly keep track of errors made by all students in the group.
- After reading, practice any difficult words.

3. Repeated Readings

a. Timed Readings

- Have individual students read the passage while other students track the text with their fingers and whisper read. Time individuals for 60 seconds. Encourage students to work for a personal best.
- For each student, count the number of words read correctly in 60 seconds (words read minus errors). Record students' scores.

b. Partner Reading—Checkout Opportunity

While students are partner reading, listen to individuals read the passage. Work on accuracy or fluency as needed.

Name_______________________________________

FLUENCY PASSAGE

The Farm

Every summer Jane and her twin sister, Jill, would 9
take a trip out of town. They would go to visit their friends 22
who lived on a farm. The twins were never bored on the 34
farm. In fact, they found it very interesting because there 44
were so many different things for them to see, hear, and 55
smell. 56

They would play around near the cows, sheep, and pigs. 66
They would listen to the odd sounds the animals made and 77
they would laugh. Some days the barnyard would be 86
smelly. That would make Jane and Jill frown. The end of 97
the summer came too quickly. The twins didn't want to 107
leave. 108

My personal best is _____ words correct per minute.

My goal is to read with 0–2 errors. This is what I did:

Reading	1st	2nd	3rd	4th
Errors				
Words/ 60 seconds				
wcpm				

Have students read the sentences. Time individual students for 60 seconds; mark errors. To determine words correct per minute (wcpm), count words read in 60 seconds, subtract errors, and record on the chart. If the student completes the passage in less than 60 seconds, have him or her return to the top and continue reading. (Repeated readings may be completed with older students, assistants, or parents.)